MOUNTAINEER

A view from the Ogre past the Latok peaks to K2.

On the North-East Ridge of Mount Everest.

CHRIS BONINGTON
MOUNTAINEER

THIRTY YEARS OF CLIMBING
ON THE WORLD'S GREAT PEAKS

DIADEM BOOKS · LONDON
AN IMPRINT OF HODDER AND STOUGHTON

Looking towards Mount Cook from the summit of Mount Tasman.

British Library and Cataloguing Data
Bonington, Chris
    Mountaineer
    1. Mountaineering. Bonington, Chris. – Biographies
    I. Title
    796.5'22'0924
    ISBN 0–906371–97–X

First published in Great Britain in 1989
by Diadem Books Ltd, London.

Trade enquiries to Hodder and Stoughton Ltd.,
Mill Road, Dunton Green, Sevenoaks, Kent TN13 2YA

Colour separations by J Film Process, Bangkok

Photoset by J&L Composition Ltd, Filey, North Yorkshire

Printed in Italy by L.E.G.O., Vicenza
on 150 gsm Gardamatt Art supplied by Cartiere del Garda, S.p.A.

ACKNOWLEDGEMENTS The author and publisher wish to thank the following for their help in
producing this volume: Margaret Body, Audrey Salkeld, Doug Scott and Louise Wilson for
editorial advice and assistance; the photographers listed below and Hilary Boardman, Carolyn
Pearce, Tom Tasker and Audrey Whillans for permission to use photographs.
    Eighty photographs taken by others are credited below [abbreviations – *2* (both pictures), *t*
(top), *b* (bottom), *i* (inset), *bl* (bottom left), *cl* (centre left) etc]: Dave Bamford 172; Pete
Boardman 125(*t*), 124(*br*), 125(*br*); Les Brown 68(*i*), 69(*br*), 70(*t, bl*), 71(*b*); Nick Colton
36(*br*); Dennis Davis 64(*tr*), 65(*r*), 69(*bl*), 70(*br*), 71(*t*); Nick Estcourt 30/31(*l*), 129, 138(*b*),
139(*l*), 140(*t*), 141(*t and i*); Tom Frost 106(*3*); Bjorn Myrer-Lund 191(*3*); Chris Ralling
120(*tr*); Dick Renshaw 166(*bl*); Ronnie Richards 99, 139(*r*); Rick Ridgeway 187(*bl,br*); Tony
Riley 146, 149(*bl*); Henry Rogers 10(2), 11; Doug Scott 116(*br*), 117(*bl*), 118(*3*), 119(*bl*),
122(*bl*), 124(*t,bl*), 142(*br*), 143(*b*); Clive Rowland 142(*bl*), 144(*bc*), 145(*tr,i,br*); Joe Tasker
33(*main shot*), 148(*b*), 149(*bl*); Derek Walker 73(*tl,tc,tr,cr*); Don Whillans 26(*r*), 29(*b*), 43(*bl*),
75(*br*), 76(*tl,cl*), 77(*bl*); David Wilson 155(*br*); Ken Wilson 63(*r*), 66/67, 113(*i,br*), 114/115,
116(*t*), 119(*t*), 121(*t*); Keiichi Yamada 110.

CONTENTS

The ice-field below the Central Couloir
of the Grandes Jorasses.

Introductory Note

by Ken Wilson

Since the beginnings of the sport of mountaineering in the last century thousands of books have been written by those seeking to describe its great adventure and the imposing surroundings in which it takes place. There has been no more active exponent of this tradition than Chris Bonington who has recorded his many great ascents in nine books (three autobiographies and six expedition accounts). Bonington's climbs include some of the most eventful in the history of the sport. The straight record disguises the drama – the risk of the Nally rescue on the Eiger, the driving ambition to make the first ascent of the Frêney Pillar, the organisational energy required to bring off the Annapurna and Everest face climbs, the remorseless push that placed him on the summit of the Ogre and the survival instincts that got him and Doug Scott off the mountain. On Kongur, four battle-hardened climbers pressed on tenaciously to force a conclusion. On Shivling an inspired climb was snatched in swashbuckling style. It is a record replete with incident, tragedy and adventure.

Yet in Bonington's books, as in those of his celebrated predecessors, Whymper, Shipton and Smythe, perhaps a key element is missing. The sheer scale and majesty of the surroundings in which the adventures have taken place has remained curiously unfocussed, hinted at maybe in a few telling photographs, but never really developed in visual terms. We may have penetrating word pictures, but the illustrations remain subordinated to the text, their potential to add to our understanding underexploited.

Although others have depicted mountain architecture, texture and ecology, very few books have been published that illustrate comprehensively the mountaineering struggle in its tight arena of stark challenging savagery, and provide some hint of the sheer scale of the peaks and a feeling for their moods – the rumble of afternoon avalanches, the flash and crack of an incipient thunder storm. Chris Bonington covers this territory frequently in his lectures and now at last he has assembled from his many photographs this permanent visual record of his major ascents, in some ways a superior photo-album, but also a portfolio that may offer new clues about why mountaineers pursue their strange but compelling sport. The price is often high – the book covers several fatal accidents – but the rewards are great too. The satisfaction of a high mountain climbed by a powerful route is profound and long-lasting. It is the nature of this challenge which this book addresses, and possibly, through Chris Bonington's life, we may derive a greater understanding of instincts that may reside, in some form, in us all.

I   Foundations

I stopped, found a crack for a belay and pulled up over the top of the crag. It was a cold grey January day in the indifferent winter of 1989, and Graham Little, my partner, and I were putting up a first winter ascent on a Scottish crag just south of Glen Coe. As he climbed up to join me it suddenly struck me that it was thirty-six years since I had first climbed in Scotland in the fresh excited dawn of my long love for the mountains. I gazed out over the vast stretch of the Rannoch Moor, a patchwork of black open lochans against the grey dusting of snow, whilst to the north lay the white piles of the Mamores, Ben Nevis part hidden in cloud, and the peaks of Glen Coe.

I loved what I saw and felt the contentment that comes from overcoming doubt and fear. I had been where no-one had ever been before and had touched rock and frozen moss that had never known a human hand. It didn't matter that the climb was not my discovery but Graham's. I could pick out Buachaille Etive Mor away in the distance across the wide expanse of peat and water and I recalled that from the flanks of the Buachaille the empty sweep of the Moor had had the same magical fascination and I had experienced the same doubts and fears those many years ago as I followed Hamish MacInnes, already established as one of Scotland's best climbers, up Agag's Groove and Raven's Gully, both of them first winter ascents well beyond my experience at the time.

From those early beginnings to the present day my essential motives for climbing have remained the same. Climbing on British crags in winter and summer is the foundation of our sport, though perhaps "way of life" is a more apt description. This activity of ours influences so much of our lives.

For me it started with a feeling for wild places, long walks in the Quantocks in Somerset and then in the Wicklow Hills, where I spent parts of a couple of summer holidays with my grandfather at Black Rock, a suburb of Dublin. On the way back to London by Holyhead in Anglesey, I was intrigued by the sight of valleys winding mysterious, into the high, grass-clad Welsh hills. They were the Carnedds, though I didn't know it at the time. I then stumbled across a picture book of the Scottish Highlands. I had never been north of the border but was fascinated by the scale of the mountains and the thought of wandering amongst them.

My first real mountain adventure was in Snowdonia in the New Year of 1951 when I hitch-hiked there with a friend and we were caught in a small avalanche.

There is no more satisfying experience in British climbing than doing a big rock climb on a high mountain crag on a warm summer's day. The great North Face of Scafell is perhaps the most traditional of such crags, offering a range of routes of all grades established since the beginnings of the sport. All are worthwhile. Jones's Route of 1898 on the Pinnacle Face (*right*) is a fine Severe, Fred Botterill's famous slab climb is a classic Very Severe first climbed in 1903. It was here that Siegfried Herford climbed the Great Flake of Central Buttress in 1914. Nick Estcourt and I added White Wizard to the crag in 1971 which, though unfortunately flawed by some aid points, was soon led free to make one of the best and, at E3, more demanding climbs on the cliff.

Geoff Francis and I made an early ascent of Cemetery Gates in the Llanberis Pass in 1954. The protection was so sparse that Geoff thought it was best to split the big pitch and I led through up the hard crack to the ledge.

Soloing Hangover on Harrison's Rocks in 1955.

Soon after I was introduced to rock climbing at Harrison's Rocks, the sandstone outcrop south of London, and later in Llanberis, and I spent some of the long summer holidays discovering Scotland.

I was building the foundations of an activity that has filled my life ever since and enabled me to achieve what I have. The elation at being on a steep crag with the added spice of risk is something that has never left me. I revelled in climbing on loose rock with little protection. It was all a process of discovery. It didn't matter that I was repeating someone else's route. For me it was a fresh and new experience. I was constantly extending my own ability. The beauty of the mountains was also immensely important, that very beauty enhanced by the scale of the commitment.

One of my strongest memories of those early days was an ascent of the West Buttress of Suilven in the Northern Highlands. It juts in isolated splendour above a rolling glaciated rock base, a great whaleback of a mountain that looks much taller than its modest 2398ft/731m. We left our rucksacks at the foot of the West Buttress, traversed the mountain, and then picked them up to walk south along the shores of Loch Sionascaig towards Stac Pollaidh, whose cock's-comb of sandstone pinnacles dominated the southern horizon. That long summer's day, that stretched into the night, had everything that takes me back to the mountains year after year. There was also the drive of competition. Having found something I was good at, I inevitably measured myself against others, whether it was on some light-hearted bouldering or the search for a new route. This competitive element was not all-important but it was certainly a strong one.

Climbing in the early fifties was not very different from what it had been before the Second World War. My first rope was of pre-war hemp. I had a pair of clinker nailed boots and used gym shoes on the harder climbs. A couple of hemp slings was all I had for running belays. I persuaded my mother to buy me a nylon rope after I had been climbing a year and carried a selection of nylon slings — line to slide round tiny flakes and full weight to go over bollards. It wasn't just that the hills were less full than they are now, there was a lack of communication between different climbing groups. There were no national climbing magazines and mountaineering was rarely touched by the national press. There were rumours of a talented group of Manchester climbers, whose leaders were Joe Brown and Don Whillans, but they had a myth-like quality, the difficulty of the routes they were putting up being exaggerated by the lack of information.

My first big fall was in 1952 on Scar's Climb on the Terrace Wall of the East Face of Tryfan in Snowdonia. At that stage it had never occurred to me that I could fall. The route followed a thin finger-width crack that petered out towards its top after about thirty feet. I had draped a few line slings over tiny flakes and kept going even though the holds were running out, until a foot slewed off. I toppled backwards and was conscious of plunging head first down the crag, to come back to consciousness at the bottom with a bloody head and sprained ankle. I managed to hobble back down, supported by some climbers and walkers who had seen the fall, and was given a lift to the doctor in Bethesda who patched me up and I hitch-hiked home the following day, very

aware that I was not infallible.

Climbing in Britain in summer and winter filled my horizon into the mid-fifties. The announcement, on a windy parade ground at Royal Air Force Hednesford, of the first ascent of Everest on the day of the Coronation, had a remote quality that hardly moved me. Even the Alps were beyond me in terms of distance and cost. My challenges were closer to home; my first visit to Clogwyn Du'r Arddu, my first Very Severe then Extreme lead, which was Spectre on Clogwyn y Grochan (since dropped to Hard VS). But the greatest challenge was our opening of the Main Wall of the Avon Gorge. I was a cadet at Sandhurst at the time and the Avon Gorge gave us the most accessible climbing at weekends. We quickly exhausted the existing routes on the buttress to the side of the main quarried area. The Main Wall was about 200 feet high, with few lines of weakness and the rock looked suspect. It held both the fascination yet intimidation of the unknown, in the unlikely setting of the city of Bristol with traffic roaring below and the suburb of Clifton above. There is a cave at the foot of the face where we often bivouacked, so perhaps familiarity with that particular bit of rock led us to

An early attempt on Mercavity which we eventually climbed in 1955. In hindsight our new routes in the Avon Gorge were extremely adventurous undertakings. The quarried Main Wall didn't offer many spikes for slings or cracks for chockstones. We therefore had to rely on soft steel pitons for runners. On Malbogies I had just two pitons for protection on the first pitch and a draped sling on the second.

make our first attempt on an unlikely bulging wall to its immediate right. I was with Geoff Francis, a medical student, with whom I had done some of my best climbing. We skirmished on the bottom few feet for a couple of weekends before I summoned up the courage to commit myself to the climb, pulling over an overhang about twenty feet up without any runners. The rock was dubious and there were no cracks for pitons. There was now no question of turning back and we picked our way delicately through the overlapping holdless slabs that are so characteristic of the Avon Gorge. It's a style of climbing that I have always revelled in. There were few runners, even less than there are today and some very loose rock in places and yet it was a superb route with all the thrill of being the first on a large expanse of rock. We made three more ascents on the Main Wall in the next couple of years but it was to be at least five

Martin Boysen leading the second pitch of the Medlar, Raven Crag, Thirlmere during our first ascent in 1964. A month later I added Totalitarian on the same crag with Mike Thompson.

years before any of them was repeated and further routes were made on the Wall.

Another memorable venture was in 1960 when I climbed for the first time with Tom Patey, one of the most prolific and colourful characters of the post-war Scottish scene, climbing ten new routes across the North-West in as many days. They varied from the classic Cioch of Applecross, an improbable V. Diff. that soars up a spectacular sandstone nose, to King Cobra on the Coireachan Ruadh Face on the Main Ridge of the Cuillins in Skye that took this magnificent wall by its most direct line. Climbing with Patey was a magical mystery tour of superb unclimbed lines in the mountains of the west and ceilidhs at the other side of the country after a long day's climbing. He soloed at about the same standard he led and all too often a climb became a race to catch up with him to persuade him to put on the rope. Tom was particularly interested in sea stacks and master-minded the first ascents of many of the most famous ones – the Old Man of Stoer, the Stack of Handa and, of course, the celebrated Old Man of Hoy.

My bible and inspiration at this time was W. H. Murray's *Mountaineering in Scotland*. The climbs described in it were within my sight, that I could dream of attaining and, in the process, I was building the solid foundations of experience that were to stand me in good stead when I was ready for the next adventure further afield.

But even after reaching the Alps and then the greater ranges, British climbing has been something that I have always cherished, and of which I have never tired. I suppose I reached my own peak in terms of technical ability from around the mid-fifties to mid-sixties. I was climbing the most difficult routes of the day, making second ascents of the hardest Brown routes, such as Surplomb, Woubits and the Mostest, and putting up hard new routes particularly in the Avon Gorge and Cheddar. The highest standard of the time was Extremely Severe which by modern standards would rate around E2. I've managed to hold that standard into the present day, even leading the occasional E3. I've abandoned competition with others but still enjoy competing with myself.

The sport itself is in a constant state of development and change. The climbing explosion of the late forties and early fifties, led by Joe Brown and Don Whillans, was very directly facilitated by the increased prosperity of the post-war era, combined with the five-day week. It meant that young working-class lads could get out, first onto the grit, and then to North Wales and the Lakes. The very fact that they had manual jobs, in Don and Joe's case, plumbing, meant they had physical strength without recourse to training.

The next major jump forward in climbing standards was that of the mid-seventies, led to a large degree by Peter Livesey. It was he who introduced the concept of training for climbing, bringing a more disciplined and systematic approach to the activity. There was at the same time a change in attitude. The free-wheeling approach of the sixties and early seventies, highlighted by legendary tales of Llanberis drugs and booze and all-night parties, was replaced with the more serious, achievement-orientated, atmosphere of the eighties. Another influence was the extent to which every available piece of rock was being climbed. Each generation needs to find new challenges and new ground and, as the lines following features which can yield protection are climbed, the pioneer is forced onto places where there is no natural means of protection.

This advance in standards has been accompanied by the development of

(right) The South Face of the Old Man of Hoy with the East Face in shadow on the right. On the third day of the first ascent we regained our high point by a wild pendulum and jumar up the overhanging crack *(above)*.

THE OLD MAN OF HOY, 1966

Tom Patey's finest rock climbing discovery was a route up this famous sea stack in the Orkneys. The stack took three days to climb. Tom conducted proceedings with Rusty Baillie and me forming an admiring chorus, Rusty leading the main overhanging crack pitch, such was Tom's generosity. We returned in 1967 to make a televised ascent with an all-star cast that included Joe Brown, Ian McNaught Davis, Dougal Haston and Pete Crew who climbed the ridges flanking the South Face, while Tom and I repeated our East Face line which, following the TV programme, soon achieved classic status.

Malham Cove, a beautiful limestone crag in the depths of the Yorkshire Dales, offers some of the hardest modern testpieces set alongside equally fine climbs in a more traditional mould.

Don Whillans and I in 1983, equipped fifties-style for a commemoration ascent of Dovedale Grooves. It was to be the last time that I climbed with my doughty partner of many an alpine adventure.

Nick Escourt, my regular partner in the seventies, leading Sidewalk on Dow Crag.

CLIMBING IN BRITAIN

The joy of climbing in Britain is based on its diversity of cliffs, all the more valuable for being in close proximity to most of the major centres of population. Limestone and gritstone cliffs peep from many Pennine valleys, austere mountain crags made from various attractive types of igneous rock are found in abundance in Wales, the Lake District and Scotland. There are sea cliffs, quarries, sandstone outcrops and bouldering areas. In winter Scotland can always be counted on to provide tremendous ice climbing.

Then there is the never ending variety of who one climbs with — regular partners, novices, young thrusting hot shots, chance acquaintances, seasoned old campaigners — their zest for the sport enhances the experience of the climb topped off, invariably, with a pint at the nearest pub.

Creag Meaghaidh at dawn (*below*). This is one of the best cliffs in Scotland for winter climbing and North Post (*right*), which I climbed with Jim Fotheringham, is one of its finest climbs.

artificial protection. It's part of the constant dialogue between the thrill of risk and the desire to hedge one's bets, to reduce that risk in the event of a fall. This is the area of ethical argument that has accompanied climbing from its earliest days. In the thirties, and going on through to the sixties, it was the question of the piton and whether to use it or not. Continental climbers embraced its use from the late twenties. With the greater scale of the Alps and the need for haste, there was never time for quite so many ethics. Not only did the British abhor the piton, there was a distrust and misunderstanding of the bold style of alpinism, particularly on the big limestone walls of the Austrian Alps and Dolomites, being practised by young German, Austrian and Italian climbers. Our own little crags in Britain were not suited to such a cavalier approach. We could afford to spend a day on a pitch and if we hammered a piton into a crack every time the mouse of fear nibbled, the spice of risk would have been banished.

But as climbing standards increased, the tempation to use pitons became greater. Alongside this, British climbers were using continental methods in the Alps. They were climbing the aid routes of the Dolomites, and then trying out the same techniques on the limestone crags of Derbyshire and Yorkshire. It was exciting and fun. I can still remember the thrill of heaving up on

White Noise (E3) on Recastle Crag near Keswick. Leading a hard pitch like this is a fascinating exercise. After fixing runners, some of questionable security, up the lower wall, an exploratory peep up the hard section reveals another welcome runner point. Then a contrived rest before the big push — the initial committing move, then forcing steadily upwards, arms and fingers tiring, but hopefully staying in enough control to gain another resting point and with luck another runner. The possibility of failure and a fall or desperate retreat is ever present, adding the spice of danger that makes success correspondingly sweet.

rusty pegs under Kilnsey's main overhang — incredible to think that it has now been climbed free.

There always was a resistance to the use of pitons, a feeling of abuse at metal being hammered into cracks, so less intrusive means of protection were sought. The development of protection from the sling placed over a spike of rock and a pocketful of pebbles to insert into cracks, through the first drilled out nuts to the sophisticated curved wedges and camming devices of today, reflects this search. The modern nuts and camming devices are very versatile and reduce routes that had a high level of risk back in the early sixties to relatively safe technical exercises and yet there is a satisfaction in the ingenuity required to get good nut placements. For a start you need the natural feature; you then need to select the right device and place it carefully with sensitivity rather than force, even if you give the nut a good tug to make sure it is secure.

But today there is a problem. Since most of the major natural lines to the very highest level of difficulty have been climbed, talented young climbers, out to extend themselves and establish their own identity, are forced onto stretches of rock where there is little or no natural protection. A few have continued to explore under the old terms, putting up routes where a fall would be long and possibly fatal, but a growing number of climbers now prefer to shorten the odds and opt for a well placed bolt. Once bolts are drilled indiscriminately the natural features of the rock become meaningless. A route can go anywhere, particularly if the climber is also prepared to chip the odd hold where nature has failed to provide one. The whole element of adventure and exploration, of being attuned to the natural environment is replaced by an approach that is more gymnastic in keeping with the trend that climbing has taken in recent years with its emphasis on training, its use of artificial climbing walls and the development of competition climbing.

There is a fear that the ethos of British climbing, that had developed over the years from the time when our Victorian forebears started exploring vegetated gullies in Snowdonia and the Lake District, will be destroyed. I am more sanguine. There will be changes and there will be an increasing pressure to fill in the gaps between natural lines with yet more routes protected by bolts, but there will also be argument in the pub and in the pages of the climbing press, and through this I think a balance will be found. Some athletic climbers might become divorced from the game that I know, but many more will continue to enjoy the crags, pushing themselves to limits of their own choice, balancing out the thrill of risk, the desire for self-preservation, the satisfaction of physical expression and a love for the natural environment.

Living on the northern edge of the Lake District I have two dozen good crags within easy reach for a quick climb. Here Doug Scott, fellow expeditioner, and neighbour, coils the rope after an evening ascent at Sandbed Ghyll near Castle Rock, Thirlmere.

2 The Alpine Experience

The Alps have a perfect scale, high enough to hold the snows and glaciers, yet not so high that every step is an effort as you struggle against the rarified air. From the granite spires and ridges of the Mont Blanc massif to the limestone of the Oberland and the chaotic towers and walls of the Dolomites, their variety of rock, snow and ice, their bergschrunds and crevasses, stonefall and sudden fierce changes of weather make them an ideal training ground for the bigger mountains of Asia, but also the epitome of adventurous climbing in themselves.

My first alpine season was in 1957 with Hamish MacInnes. He was already very experienced and had ambitious plans for us. Hamish's knowledge of the Eastern Alps had led him to explore new techniques, particularly the use of pitons, not only for protection, but also for direct aid – a development still frowned on by the British climbing establishment, but one which had made possible such hallmarks of the era as the first ascent of the West Face of the Petit Dru, and Bonatti's remarkable solo ascent of the South-West Pillar.

The first alpine hut I ever stayed in was the ruined Refuge de Leschaux, a battered relic that was a fitting launch point for the North Wall of the Grandes Jorasses and those other magnificent and lonely peaks at the head of the Leschaux Glacier. Its spartan solitude was very different from the more popular areas with their crowded huts and queues of climbers that I became familiar with in the following years. But there is an anticipatory excitement in a crowded hut, in its babel of different languages, chance encounters with old acquaintances swilling wine and coffee, the packed communal bunks and the intensity of the early morning start. Then once outside, the crunch of crampons in crisp frozen snow, the little chains of light scattering towards the dark loom and serrated silhouette of the peaks, the intensity of the black of the sky and the brilliance of the stars. Fears that had slipped around the mind insidiously overnight, vanish in the urgency of movement, to be replaced by a heady excitement at what the day will bring. It's the rhythm of movement that makes climbing in the Alps so satisfying: the approach by the light of a head torch, arrival at the start in the dawn, then climbing up into the heat of the sun. Even a difficult route, requiring belays, builds a rhythm of steady movement, setting up the belay with minimum delay, a pause to contemplate the expanding vision of mountains and glacier, as your partner climbs up and through, time to assess the patterns of cloud – a frisson of fear, is it going to change?

The magnificent rock wall of the West Face of the Petit Dru, overlooking Chamonix, throws down an irresistible challenge. Climbs are both technical and serious as they must be approached by the stone-raked Dru couloir which slants up below the face. The Dru symbolised modern alpinism in the fifties and sixties and it was here that Yosemite big-wall techniques found their natural expression in the Alps.

Mick Burke, seen in this photo, a member of my Annapurna and Everest teams of the seventies, was something of a Dru expert. With Gary Hemming and René Desmaison, he took part in the audacious Dru rescue of two stricken German climbers in 1966 in the days before helicopters were able to pluck beleaguered climbers from the face.

The ruined Leschaux Hut with the Chamonix Aiguilles in the background.

Hamish MacInnes – my alpine mentor. He introduced me to alpine climbing in 1957 and we climbed together again in 1958.

It's the epics you remember most vividly: the South-West Pillar of the Petit Dru, my first serious climb, with Hamish concussed by stonefall on the first bivouac, and the storm that caught us just below the top. The primitive gear we used then ensured bivouacs were chilly affairs, the only concession to warmth being a light down jacket and a large poly bag. The retreat Rusty Baillie and I had from the Right-Hand Pillar of Brouillard in a violent storm was potentially very dangerous and, after a precarious bivouac threatened by lightning and pounded by spindrift avalanches, should have been desperately uncomfortable, but strangely it wasn't. During the night we had managed to keep warm, brewed up occasionally and chatted companionably. In the morning we began our retreat down rocks plastered in fresh snow. We had no abseiling devices in 1965; it was the old shoulder and karabiner abseil, difficult to control with icy ropes. We had no contact. Even standing side by side we could hardly hear what the other said because of the scream of the wind. We had never climbed together before that summer and were temperamentally very different, but in the face of extreme danger our combined abilities and experience had complemented each other in concentration on survival, picking the right line and ensuring that the rope didn't snag when we pulled it down.

Back in the valley, we shared a sense of absolute satisfaction, and appreciated living because we had taken ourselves to the very brink but had remained masters of the situation. Rather than fight the elements, we had worked with them. The experience had increased our confidence, and all we wanted was to return and finish a route we had so very nearly completed.

Having turned back only a few yards from the top of the Pillar, it could be argued that we had discovered all there was to be found, even if we couldn't claim the first ascent for the guide books. A great deal of my alpine climbing in the sixties was involved in what became races to be first – the Central Pillar of Frêney, first British ascent of the North Wall of the Eiger and the Eiger Direct. I enjoyed the race. I had already discovered on British rock just how competitive I was. But although I am spurred by a sense of competition and thoroughly enjoy winning, it is not the prime motivation. I wanted to climb the North Wall of the Eiger as a test of my all round mountaineering ability, for I believe it is the supreme measure of alpine skill.

Alpinism is the crucible of mountaineering sense and judgement, of picking a safe line, judging stonefall, assessing the weather, deciding whether to go on or retreat. So many of these decisions are made on a gut intuition. When Ian Clough and I climbed the Walker Spur of the Grandes Jorasses in 1962, we bivouacked at its foot with twelve other parties. Next morning we started jockeying to get past them, and then, as a threatening bank of cloud swept in from the west, everyone else turned back. Yet it never occurred to Ian or myself to do so. Being sure of each other and our ability to cope if the weather did break, we pressed on to enjoy what turned into a perfect day.

Good climbing partnerships are the key to alpine success, as they are based on levels of communication that are anticipatory. There is very little need for discussion of the route, or even fundamental issues like whether to go on or back. You can concentrate on looking after yourself, because you know that your partner is doing the same. Yet very few such relationships are completely equal; there is nearly always an edge of stronger will or greater experience which influences how decisions are made. The long-lasting partnerships are ones where the imbalance is accepted and those that break up are usually where there is a change in this status.

I was lucky to have my most intense years of alpinism through the late fifties and sixties. There was still a wealth of major unclimbed lines to be tackled and the Alps had a feeling of size and seriousness that has certainly been eroded in recent times, due to improvements in equipment, the development of helicopter rescue, and basic changes in perception. Today there is a good chance of being plucked from half-way up the North Wall of the Eiger and many other of the great faces if something goes wrong, whereas before helicopter rescue was perfected, escaping from a dangerous face could be a desperate business.

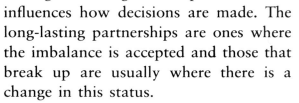

Hamish MacInnes in action on the South East Spur of the Pointe de Lepiney in 1957. We had nearly completed the route when a wooden wedge came out. I fell and we abandoned the attempt.

Descent from the Brouillard Face after a storm.

The change in perception is demonstrated by the leading alpinists of today. Climbing achievement is increasingly measured in a combination of speed, difficulty and quantity: Christophe Profit, for instance, soloing the North Faces of the Eiger, Jorasses and Matterhorn in the space of twenty-four hours, using a helicopter to travel between the peaks, or the increasing use of parapentes by alpinists to assist in rapid descent during multi-route extravaganzas. These sort of achievements call upon an extraordinary level of skill, stamina, and risk acceptance. Yet for all this dazzling brilliance, climbers who reach this level of ability miss out on the romance of exploratory discovery.

The modern rock climbing developments in the Mont Blanc massif on peaks like the Aiguille du Midi, the Grand Capucin and the West Face of the Blaitiere are both impressive and fun. Where we clomped ponderously in mountain boots, heaving a rucksack and making a bivouac almost inevitable because of the amount we were carrying, today's rock climber, with sticky rubber climbing shoes and a rack of modern nuts and camming devices, races up in a matter of hours. The experience is great, and yet something of the scale and majesty of the Alps is lost. I wonder how many of the younger climbers miss out the classic routes altogether, in their concentration on modern rock routes in the high mountain areas.

The last time I climbed in the Alps we tackled two classic Grade 6 rock climbs in remote areas and we had them to ourselves. Looking at the hut book, they were not climbed as often as would have been expected. After these we turned to the Eisnaze on the Piz Scerscen, followed by a traverse to the Piz Bernina, descending the Biancograt. The route had been first climbed in 1887, and had no technically difficult climbing, but there was smooth fifty-degree ice on the way to the Piz Scerscen, a knife-edged rock ridge, with endless rocky gendarmes, from which escape would have been difficult, giving it a seriousness that is lacking in many modern rock climbs on the Mont Blanc massif. We had the mountain to ourselves and enjoyed a perfect day steeped in the tradition of the founders of our sport. I could imagine our Victorian forebears with their great long alpenstocks, and clinker-nailed boots, straddling the knife-edged ridge. There was continuous movement, decisions about route finding, the vista of the mountains around us, an exhausted stumbling return in the dark and the absolute luxury of huge plates of pasta washed down by wine in the hut. That week brought home to me the variety of challenge, enjoyment and adventure that is encompassed in our familiar and much abused Alps of Western Europe. This familiarity may have blinded us to the compact diversity of these mountains but for me, and I suspect for thousands of other climbers, alpinism is very much alive.

PETIT DRU, SOUTH-WEST PILLAR, 1958

Hamish MacInnes and I wanted to make the first British ascent, as did Don Whillans and Paul Ross, so we joined forces. The route was bigger and more serious than anything I had previously tackled. We just avoided a huge rock avalanche in the approach couloir but during the first bivouac Hamish was injured in a stonefall. Fearing a descent of the couloir we felt it best to go on and, with Hamish a casualty, the rest of the climb became a struggle – with two extra bivouacs, a shortage of food and then a storm. I learnt a great deal from Don Whillans during this epic. It was his drive and leadership that got us up the route.

Petit Dru, South-West Pillar – Whillans off route on the lower section leading a desperate crack.

Hamish MacInnes injured and groggy after being hit by a stone.

PETITES JORASSES, WEST FACE

After the Dru I teamed up with Ronnie Wathen to make the first British ascent (fourth overall) of this fine rock face, which commands good views of the Walker Spur. The climb was all the sweeter as we beat the 'Rock and Ice' stalwarts Whillans, Hadlum and Smith to it by a day.

(*right*) The West Face of the Petites Jorasses – I am jubilant after leading the crux overhang which looked hard but proved to be a delight to climb.

The view of the Grandes Jorasses from the Couvercle Hut. The Petites Jorasses is on the left and the Rochefort Ridge the skyline on the right.

Approaching the Grey Tower on the Walker Spur.

GRANDES JORASSES, THE WALKER SPUR, 1962

The Petites Jorasses climb had given us a grandstand view of the Walker Spur and had left me with a yearning ambition to tackle this most elegant of all the great north face routes. I was lucky to team up with Ian Clough to snatch the climb at the end of the eventful 1962 season. At the foot of the spur we found several other parties with the same idea and were soon jostling for position on the lower rocks. But the weather looked threatening and all the other parties turned back. Ian and I felt so confident and fit that it never occurred to us to retreat. Our intuitive feeling proved to be correct, the weather cleared, and we were able to make a fast

Ian Clough on the ridge of the Grandes Jorasses, near Pointe Hélène

Lunch of abandoned spaghetti at the Canzio Bivouac Hut on the Col des Grandes Jorasses.

ascent and reached the summit in the afternoon.

In the euphoria of our rapid climb we opted to bivouac on the summit, and next day, in blustery but sunny conditions traversed all the summits of the Jorasses and the Rochefort Ridge to reach the Torino Hut and complete a magnificent expedition. We had intended to cap this success by returning to Chamonix via the Brenva Face of Mt Blanc, but with the weather still good it was clear that there was only one climb to go for – the Eiger North Wall!

(*right*) The Walker Spur, less steep than it appears from the Couvercle, is approached across a complex glacier and initial ice slopes that are exposed to stonefall.

Don Whillans on the West Face of the Aiguille Noire de Peuterey (*above*) with the Frêney Face beyond; (*right*) I tackle one of the key pitches high on the route with combined aid and free techniques.

EQUIPMENT AND TACTICS

Choice of equipment for an alpine climb is a source of constant debate. We climbed everything in boots and only hauled our sacks on the most difficult ground. We used North Wall hammers and daggers for ice work. Crash helmets were just coming into vogue, though Whillans preferred his cloth cap stuffed with padding. He was attracted to direct lines on big mountains and was not interested in a new route if it failed to match this criterion.

Tom Patey – always on the lookout for new routes.

One classic route that I climbed with him was the West Face of the Aiguille Noire, a testing rock climb on the wild and serious south side of Mont Blanc.

Tom Patey and Joe Brown preferred new routes, however obscure, and they kept a list of possibilities in a black ledger. They made a strong team, specialising in fast one-day ascents carrying minimal gear, with Joe always available to lead a problematic rock pitch. In 1964 (with Robin Ford) I joined them on a couple of first ascents on the Chamonix Aiguilles.

A typical campsite scene before a big climb – the gear is laid out, packed, unpacked, thinned, and packed again in a repeated attempt to reduce weight.

Tom Patey tests the strength of my brand new continental helmet with his MacInnes North Wall hammer.

(*left*) Joe Brown during the first ascent of the North Face of Pointe Migot, sporting a makeshift crash helmet – a precursor of the famous Joe Brown helmet that he introduced in the seventies?

Attempting the Fissure Brown.

AIGUILLE DE BLATIERE, WEST FACE, 1961

The first ascent of this testing rock climb in 1954 by Don Whillans and Joe Brown signaled a resurgence of British climbing in the Alps. Ian Clough and I wanted to do it as a training climb before the Frêney Pillar. The Fissure Brown – one of the hardest pitches – was normally protected by large wooden wedges but we found these had been removed and I was faced with a fiendish off-width crack as hard as one of Brown's difficult gritstone climbs. My attempts in bendy boots and with no protection resulted in dismal failure and we retreated. In the meantime the other members of our team, Don Whillans and Jan Djuglosz, had become impatient and decided to set off without us, but at the Col de la Fourche Djuglosz felt ill and they too had to return. Their misfortune, our good luck!

The southern flank of Mont Blanc from the summit of the Aiguille Noire showing the Frêney Pillars (centre) with the Brouillard Face beyond the Col Eccles on the left.

The French team, heavily laden, at the téléphérique station.

MONT BLANC: THE CENTRAL PILLAR OF FRÊNEY, 1961

Guarded by some of the steepest and most chaotic glaciers in the Alps, Mont Blanc's South Face has an almost Himalayan scale. Its most challenging unclimbed line was the great central rock spur above the Frêney Glacier that had already repulsed several attempts, most notably, earlier in that season, a seven-strong Franco–Italian team led by Walter Bonatti and Pierre Mazeaud. They had tried to sit out a storm near the top of the Pillar but were eventually forced back – four of the party died from exposure and exhaustion during a harrowing descent. After a summer of Eiger-waiting Don Whillans and I had returned to Chamonix to attempt the Central Pillar. We invited René Desmaison to join us but he declined and we therefore joined up with Ian Clough and Jan Djuglosz. When we arrived at the téléphérique Desmaison, Pierre Julien and Yves Poulet Villard were there, obviously prepared for a serious climb – it could only be the Central Pillar! So the race was on.

CENTRAL PILLAR (continued)

The Frêney Pillar is situated in a most inaccessible position high on Mont Blanc and can be approached in three possible ways, none of them easy. In the view on the left (taken by Nick Estcourt) the climber is approaching from above the Rochers Gruber which provide a very steep direct way from the Italian side. Another Italian approach is by descending from the Col Eccles on the Innominata Ridge, just off picture on the left. The approach from the Col de Peuterey (leading in from the right of the picture) is the only feasible route in France and was the one we used. It involves a night approach across the Brenva Glacier, followed by a steep ice face to gain the col, and then more ice slopes and a problematic bergschrund (obvious in the smaller picture) – a full climb just to reach the base of the Pillar which is at around 4000 metres. The crux is the Chandelle, the smooth pinnacle at the top. This was the obstacle that had stopped all previous attempts, its difficulty, isolation and exposure to bad weather lending the climb great seriousness and challenge.

The Central Pillar of Frêney from the Col de Peuterey.

Whillans leading one of the hard pitches on the lower part of the Pillar. (*right*) The upper part of the Central Pillar from the Peuterey Ridge.

Making the most of the sunset before an icy bivouac below the Chandelle.

CENTRAL PILLAR (continued)

Magnificent Grade 5 climbing for 600 metres led to a bivouac site at the foot of the Chandelle (*top inset*) where various relics from the previous attempt were reminders of the fate that befell Bonatti's party when the weather broke. Next day Don led up into the huge overhanging corner but had a spectacular fall out of the chimney that led through the big roof (the obvious notch in the photo opposite). Desmaison's team had caught up, and were trying to get round the Chandelle to the left. In the end I used inserted chockstones to get into the chimney and surmounted the problem. We had taken so long that we needed another bivouac. The others jumared up a rope we had dropped down the front of the pillar (this was also used by Desmaison's team the next day). When Don and I emerged on the summit of Mont Blanc we were greeted by a French journalist with a bottle of wine (*lower inset*) and realised how much interest there was in our ascent.

The key to the Chandelle – the crux move to enter the chimney.

Approaching the Pillars of Brouillard by the lower part of the Innominata Ridge route which traverses snow slopes between the ridge and the chaotic Brouilliard Glacier. The Chandelle at the top of the Frêney Pillar can be seen in profile on the right.

The Innominata Ridge above the Col de Frêney.

The final slope to the Eccles Bivouac Hut.

MONT BLANC, THE RIGHT-HAND PILLAR OF BROUILLARD, 1965

The Pillars of Brouillard, though not as high as those of Frêney, are just as remote. The approach is by the Innominata Ridge route to the Eccles Bivouac Hut and then a traverse across the upper part of the Brouillard Glacier. In the mid-sixties only the Left-Hand (Red) Pillar had been climbed (Bonatti and Oggioni, 1959). Rusty Ballie and I made three attempts on the Right-Hand Pillar in 1965. The first failed after we dropped the stove and ran short of pitons. On our second attempt, though we forgot nearly all our food, we pressed on and had almost completed the climb when a fierce storm forced us to make a desperate abseil retreat down icy ropes to regain the haven of the Eccles Hut. This high hut makes the Brouillard routes slightly less serious than those of the Frêney.

Tending the stove in the Eccles Hut.

(*right*) A view of the Pillar from the approach above the Eccles Hut. We followed a diagonal line up the slabs towards obvious slanting dièdre.

The lower part of the Pillar during our second attempt, with the storm brewing over Italy.

THE RIGHT-HAND PILLAR
OF BROUILLARD, (continued)

On our third attempt we were joined by Brian Robertson and John Harlin. With our knowledge of the route, we made fast progress, climbing the lower part of the Innominata Ridge to the Eccles Hut in one afternoon. After a magnificent climb up marvellous granite cracks and dièdres we reached the top of the Pillar the following day but as we moved up towards the Brouillard Ridge we were again overtaken by storm. Pressing on over Mont Blanc was out of the question and we opted instead for a bivouac and another hazardous abseil retreat to the Eccles Hut. Epics and retreats have their own peculiar charm – you always remember them more vividly than the smooth successful ascent and they make life in the valley seem even more agreeable.

Rusty Baillie following a pitch on the lower section of the Pillar. The rock was compact and the cracks rounded and deep and we used the newly introduced chrome-moly pitons repeatedly for protection and aid.

Baillie on a crack pitch leading up towards the roofs of the great dièdre – perfect granite climbing on a remote face on the highest mountain in Western Europe, the epitome alpine climbing.

(*above*) Three photos showing the retreat down the Pillar in the storm. We did not have figure-of-eight abseilers at that time and had to employ shoulder abseils which are particularly arduous on icy ropes when heavily laden. In the picture above Baillie (back to camera), Robertson and Harlin gather at the foot of the Pillar before the descent to the haven of the Eccles Hut (right).

Roping up at the foot of the Cassin route on the South Face of the Cima Piccolissima.

The overhanging north walls of the Tre Cime offer some of the greatest rock climbs of the Dolomites. Comici's famous route on the Cima Grande and Cassin's solution on the Cima Ovest were major breakthroughs in pre-war rock climbing. The *Direttissima* on the Cima Grande, first climbed in 1958 by Lother Brandler, Dieter Hasse, Jörg Lehne and Sigi Löw, was another advance in exploring ground that up to that time had seemed unclimbable.

The north faces of the Tre Cime di Lavaredo – Piccola (*left*), Grande (*centre*) and Ovest (*right*).

(*right*) A typical situation on the walls of the *Direttissima*.

The North Face of the Cima Grande with the lines of the Brandler/Hasse and Comici routes marked.

Brandler/Hasse   Comici

A view across the North Face of the Cima Grande towards the line of the *Direttissima* — the face is vertical and, at some points, overhanging.

Four photos of the ascent showing (*clockwise from above*): one of the German climbers on the lower wall; a German climber and Gunn Clark on the bivouac ledge; the aid climbing through the roofs; Gunn Clark reading the route book left on the bivouac ledge.

CIMA GRANDE, NORTH FACE DIRECT, 1959

After gazing across the huge wall during our ascent of the Comici route, Gunn Clark and I were fascinated by the *Direttissima*. We finally summoned up the courage to attempt it. The lower wall has good free climbing (with the odd aid move) and we made good progress on the first day, keeping hard on the heels of two German climbers who were on the route ahead of us. On the next day, on the big roofs, we did not do so well. We were both novices at artificial climbing, took a whole day to do two pitches, and had to bivouac again, sitting in slings just above the overhangs. The Brandler/Hasse line is a wonderful concept, however, working up the wall linking natural features in a very ingenious way – a far cry from the Saxonweg (up the wall to the left) which is a bolt ladder from bottom to top.

THE EIGER NORTH WALL
1957–1962

The 'Eigerwand', prominently situated above Kleine Scheidegg, is the most demanding of all the alpine north faces. It is a major test of mountaineering ability, demanding fitness, broad technical skill, and sound judgement. The climber must move fast, yet pace his progress up the face to avoid areas of stonefall. Weather assessment is also a factor as the Eiger is particularly prone to localised storms.

The wall is notorious for the series of accidents that took place prior to the first ascent in 1938 and it has continued to claim victims remorselessly. Many successful parties have struggled to complete the climb safely. In 1957 Hamish MacInnes and I ventured on to the face but were daunted by its scale and difficulty and retreated.

By 1961, with several hard alpine and Himalayan climbs behind me, I returned to try again in partnership with Don Whillans. We had read about the epic ascents, most notably the account in Hermann Buhl's *Nanga Parbat Pilgrimage.* Nevertheless our two attempts in 1961 came to nothing because conditions were not satisfactory.

We made another attempt in July, 1962, but were about to turn back at the start of the Second Ice-field because of stonefall, when some Swiss guides came up with news that two British climbers were in trouble further up the face. We turned round and set off across the ice-field to give them assistance.

(*left*) The North Face of the Eiger in winter. The ice-fields are tiered across the middle of the face and the Spider is inset below the summit in the centre of the circular upper wall.

Don Whillans at the Swallow's Nest bivouac.

On the Hinterstoisser Traverse.

Leaving the Swallow's Nest — Whillans on the First Ice-field using an ice peg as a dagger.

Looking down from the Second Ice-field to the guides who came to warn us of the Brewster accident.

Crossing the Second Ice-field was like going into a Second World War artillery bombardment – the entire slope was being swept by fusillades of stones. We kept going and could just discern two figures at the end of the Ice-field. Then one of them (Barry Brewster who had earlier sustained an injury) was swept away in a volley of stonefall. Luckily we were able to reach the survivor, Brian Nally, and make good our escape down the face. It was one of the most dangerous situations I have ever experienced – unjustifiable in normal circumstances and it emphasised the importance of being in the right place at the right time on such a dangerous face.

(*left*) Following a grim bivouac below the Flatiron, Brian Nally, shocked and exposed and moving like an automaton, crosses the ice slope to join us.

(*below*) Don Whillans and other Eiger aspirants waiting for suitable conditions at Kleine Scheidegg. The contrast between the dangers of the face and the pleasures below adds a curious atmosphere of unreality for those hoping to climb the route.

Crossing the Third Ice-field on our successful ascent.

Ian Clough near the top of the Ramp.

After our careful training we were nonplussed to meet these two cheerful Swiss climbers (one a virtual novice) making their third bivouac. They eventually completed the route in five days.

Moving out onto the Spider after our tactical bivouac.

THE EIGER NORTH WALL
(continued)

At the end of the 1962 season I returned with Ian Clough and made a successful ascent of the North Wall. Conditions were perfect, we were very fit and we climbed rapidly, taking care to bivouac in the late afternoon rather than risk stonefall in the Spider. The climb was a delight and, though menace was always apparent, for us it was relatively safe. Tragically, a following team was caught by stonefalls and swept from the face.

Layton Kor and John Harlin – 'the Blond God'.

THE EIGER DIRECT 1966

In the mid-sixties interest developed in the possibility of a direct route up the Eiger North Wall. John Harlin, an American living in Europe, became the driving force in the race for the climb. Harlin was known as 'the Blond God', because of his superb physique, film-star presence and his meteoric rise to the forefront of alpine climbing. Though more a mountaineer than a technical climber, he played an influential role in introducing American big-wall techniques to the Alps. I joined him in 1965 for a summer attempt, but the weather never settled and he began to plan for a winter bid. I withdrew at this point as I had no experience of alpine winter climbing and Harlin enlisted the help of Dougal Haston and the leading American rock climber, Layton Kor. The heavily publicised winter ascent of the 1938 route two years earlier had set the scene for press interest in Harlin's venture. I was asked to cover the climb as a photographer for the *Telegraph Magazine* and found myself more involved with the climbing than I had bargained for.

(*left*) Layton Kor belaying Harlin near the top of the Second Ice-field.

(*inset*) Dougal Haston, soon to become a cult figure in world climbing.

THE EIGER DIRECT
(continued)

They attempted to climb the route alpine-style, but when an eight-man German team arrived to siege the face with fixed ropes, Harlin was forced to follow suit. The Germans took the initiative, and the smaller Harlin group was stretched to keep in touch. Both teams reached the Flatiron and at this stage I was recruited to climb with Layton Kor and photographed him making the critical traverse below the Central Pillar, after which I led through up a difficult ice pitch to gain the top of the Pillar (*below*).

THE EIGER DIRECT (continued)

It was after this that the teams united
their efforts and Layton Kor and Karl
Golikow reached the Spider. Harlin and
Haston jumared up the fixed ropes to
join the Germans for the final push to
the summit. Haston reached the Spider
but Harlin was on his way up when the
rope, worn by abrasion, snapped and he
fell to his death, leaving Haston and
four of the Germans in the Spider.

John Harlin in the snow cave at the
top of the Flatiron.

(*left*) Looking down the fixed ropes
to the Central Pillar and the lower
face.

THE EIGER DIRECT, (continued)

Lehne, Strobel, Hupfauer,
Votteler and Haston fought
up the face in a violent storm
as I waited anxiously in a
snow cave on the summit to
secure the critical summit
photos. One by one they
arrived safely but caked in
ice. At Kleine Scheidegg they
faced the clamour of the
world's press. The climb had
become a piece of media
theatre, sadly magnified by
the tragedy. Yet it had been a
momentous event, in spite of
the siege tactics. If anything
the fixed ropes, which were
frighteningly insecure, added
to the seriousness. Even with
their aid, we came close to
failure and an even greater
tragedy.

It was twelve years before
'The Harlin Route' was
repeated alpine-style by Alex
MacIntyre and Tobin
Sorenson.

THE EIGER DIRECT (continued)

The final push took place during the worst storm that I have ever experienced in the mountains and most of the climbers, myself included, ended up in hospital with frostbite injuries. The climb was a harbinger for the attempts on the great faces of the Himalaya in the seventies and it also helped to open up an era of bold winter climbing in the Alps. The Eiger Direct saga was an extraordinary experience charged with terrible tragedy. One positive factor was the way that, in the face of great dangers, competition between the two teams evaporated and they worked together with great cameraderie.

Jörg Lehne and Günther Strobel, the leading pair, arrive on the summit encrusted in ice.

An hour later Dougal Haston emerged from the storm leading the second party up the ropes.

The victorious climbers pose for a celebration picture during the descent: Jörg Lehne, Günther Strobel, Roland Votteler, Dougal Haston and Siegfried Hupfauer.

Climbing the Triolet ice-field towards the headwall (*above*); mixed climbing above the ice-field (*below*); Dougal Haston (*left*) preparing for the second bivouac.

AIGUILLE DE TRIOLET, NORTH FACE DIRECT, 1975

Dougal Haston and I climbed the Triolet in January, 1975. He was very efficient and had great drive, tempered by a streak of intuitive caution. Alpine winter climbing is a fulfilling experience. We had the entire Argentière basin to ourselves. The ledges were too small to use the bivvy tent, so we slept outside, cocooned in our sleeping bags, watching the light show of a purple sunset over mountains profiled against a starlit sky. By day, as we took turns in front on steep cold rock, we were absorbed, attuned to each other and the mountains around us.

Unloading supplies on the Leschaux Glacier. The Grandes Jorasses is in the background, looking suitably threatening.

Dougal Haston using aid to overcome the bergschrund wall at the foot of the face.

GRANDES JORASSES, NORTH FACE, CENTRAL COULOIR, 1972

The then unclimbed Central Couloir is swept by stonefall in summer but Dougal Haston judged that an ice runnel on its left wall would make a superb winter route. We had decided to fly in to the head of the Leschaux Glacier to save the work of ferrying the supplies needed for a winter siege. In the event we wasted several days waiting for suitable flying conditions when, had we carried our supplies, we might have reached the top before the weather broke. The route was eventually climbed in 1976 by Alex MacIntyre and Nick Colton who climbed alpine-style in early autumn when the stonefall danger is reduced. A Japanese team sieged the main couloir two months after our failure.

Dougal Haston leading up the lower ice-field. The Japanese route goes straight up the Central Couloir, whilst our intended route was the ice runnel to the left.

(*far left*) Burke and Haston on the ice-field and at the foot of the first rock wall (*near left*).

GRANDES JORASSES (continued)

With the weather unsettled we were compelled to use siege tactics on the ice-field at the top of which Dougal and I, supported by Mick Burke and Bev Clarke, sat out a storm for three days in a tiny ice slot before making a bid for the summit. In the ice runnel we climbed two difficult rock steps, one of which entailed working bare-handed in

(*right*) Haston in the ice runnel above the first rock wall

temperatures of −20°F. At the final rock wall the weather broke, forcing us to descend. During the retreat down the fixed ropes Dougal made an error and fell out of control, but just managed to grab the rope as he did a second somersault down the ice-field. We were glad to get down alive, but we had pushed the route to our limits and were confident we could have climbed it, given one more fine day.

3 Expedition Apprenticeship

There's a smell of woodsmoke in the air and the rounded forms of the hills blur into the evening haze. My body tingles with a feeling of love for the sounds and shapes around me – a feeling of voluptuous excitement that just wants to absorb everything that is so new and strange.

That was how I felt on the first evening of our approach march to Annapurna 2 in 1960 and I still feel the same excitement at the beginning of any trip. I love the smells and sounds of the bazaar in Kathmandu, the first night away from the road under canvas, meeting old friends, drinking chang in their homes. But trekking by itself would not be enough. Once having discovered the adrenalin drive of climbing, I needed the challenge of those high mountains at the end of the walk.

Kathmandu in 1960 was a very different place. There was just one hotel, the Royal, a crumbling old Rana palace run by a White Russian called Boris. There were no tourists. Trekking had never been heard of and there was only a handful of expeditions. There were no roads outside the city and we started walking from the British Embassy.

The rhythm of the approach march has a changeless quality: the 'Cha, Sahib' of a Sherpa cookboy at dawn as a mug of tea is thrust through the tent doorway and the chatter as porters arrive. On that first trip I had a personal Sherpa to whom I handed my gear to give to the porter who would carry it. Jimmy Roberts, with his Indian Army background, knew how to manage our Sherpas. But he was devoted to them, and they to him. Being in the services we, too, accepted Jimmy's decisions as a natural extension of our service life. The fact that he was so experienced and confident, but never a martinet, undoubtedly helped. It was planning and man-management at its best. In the mid-sixties, after retiring from the Army, he founded Mountain Travel, the first of what was to become a complete industry of trekking companies, and established a tradition of service for which Nepal has become famous.

An approach march provides a delightful interval between the stresses of expedition organisation back home and the struggle on the mountain. You rarely walk more than ten miles a day, the distance a heavily laden porter can manage; you pause for lunch, prepared in the shade of a great Baobab tree by the Sherpa cook and cookboys who have raced ahead. There is time to read, talk, play cards or just absorb the feeling of the land and its people. It starts the process of

Sherpa porters at work on Annapurna 2 with the summit in the background – a typical scene from the sieged expedition of the fifties and sixties which involved the organised build up of camps, supplies and oxygen to allow a high-altitude bid for the summit. On such ventures the keynote was good leadership and teamwork with Sherpa porters playing a vital role. These easier angled routes were often serious as they are more prone to avalanches and arduous to quit after heavy snow. Flags on bamboo poles were used to mark the route and ropes were fixed on any steep sections.

The Grenfell cloth anoraks and overtrousers were windproof and functional but our rubber vapour-barrier boots, developed for duck-hunting in Alaska, whilst providing better insulation than the leather boots of the day, were hardly ideal for steep climbing.

acclimatisation to altitude and by divorcing the climber from the world he has left, helps build the team together.

In 1960 our aim was to make the first ascent of Annapurna 2. It towers massively sprawling above the Marsyandi Valley. At 26,041ft/7937m it is just below the magic 8000 metres that has become the accepted measure of the world's greatest peaks. But the way to it is long and complex, up a wide

The sights and sounds experienced on the hill paths of Nepal provide constant interest. On the Annapurna approach we passed these local musicians playing at a wedding reception.

snow buttress leading to a broad ridge that in turn leads over a shoulder, only just beneath Annapurna 4, and then on to the summit pyramid itself, in all a distance of nine kilometres. There was little physical pleasure in this long hard slog, of endless snow slopes, worries about avalanche, battering by winds and exhaustion more devastating than anything I had experienced before.

The Himalayan climber is venturing into realms where human beings were never meant to go. The highest place where people have lived all the year round is the Rongbuk Monastery in Tibet at 4950 metres, though the highest villages are around 4300 metres. It is difficult to recover from extreme fatigue above 5000 metres and at 6000 the body is progressively deteriorating. Although climbers can adjust to altitude by moving gradually up the mountain, if they stay high too long their physical deterioration can become so extreme that they no

The porter column steadily gains height in the approach to the great peaks which shimmer tantalisingly at the end of every valley.

longer function effectively. One way to avoid this is to make a series of sorties to increasing altitudes, returning in between to around 4500 metres to recuperate. Jimmy Roberts knew this and showed great wisdom in the way he planned our siege on the mountain.

Reaching the summit was of paramount importance to me. At the end of our first attempt we had one day in a storm when we tried to reach the shoulder below Annapurna 4. I

Once among the mountains their sheer scale and majesty is breathtaking. This view of Annapurnas 3, 2 and 4 from within the Annapurna Sanctuary shows our 1960 route up the obvious snow shoulder leading from the col to Annapurna 4, which we skirted to attack Annapurna 2 beyond.

Jimmy Roberts, our leader on Annapurna 2 – an exemplar of good planning and man-management.

hit a personal height barrier at 7400 metres, something I have experienced all too often since. I was not out of breath; it was as if all my strength and will had drained away. The slope was so vast that if it hadn't been for Dick Grant, out in front, I'd have given up. I would play the Himalayan target game, trying to take ten paces without a rest. I managed the eighth, the ninth, but then slumped into the snow, crying in self-pity.

We were climbing the mountain siege-style, a system developed by pre-war Everest expeditions which has been used, with variations, ever since on most of the higher mountains. It involves establishing a series of camps up the mountain, fixing ropes in position on difficult ground, until a camp is placed sufficiently close to the summit for a party to go for the top. Supplies are ferried between camps and climbers can drop back either to rest, or during bad weather, then return to the high point with comparative ease.

High-altitude porters performed a vital role in this operation. Sherpas were first employed by pre-war Everest expeditions who hired them on their way through Darjeeling, where there was a large Sherpa community. They came from Sola Khumbu, on the south side of Everest and, although of Tibetan origin, had developed their own very individual character and customs. At home they subsistence farmed, and carried trade goods between India and Tibet. This gave them an adventurous and entrepreneurial quality that enabled them to develop from being outstanding high-altitude porters to running their own prosperous

The high pastures above Sola Khumbu on the approach to Nuptse where the Sherpas take their yaks for summer grazing. The spectacular twin-topped Kang Taiga (22,241ft/ 6779m) is one of many shapely peaks that flank the valley.

tourist industry in the seventies. I quickly learnt to appreciate the Sherpas' rich sense of humour, sound common sense, courage and determination.

Climbing alpine-style is undoubtedly less monotonous and more fun. You load your sack in the valley with food, gear and bivouac equipment, walk to the foot of the climb and then keep going, carrying everything with you, to the top of the mountain and back. This style of climbing had been employed on 6000 metre peaks and in 1957 a small party of Austrians led by Marcus Schmuck, which included Hermann Buhl, climbed Broad Peak (26,400ft/8047m) using this technique. The three previous attempts on Annapurna 2 had all been small and used light-weight siege tactics. One had reached the shoulder below Annapurna 4 but been daunted by the remaining distance to the main peak. Jimmy Roberts, with a comparatively weak and inexperienced team, was taking no risks. We were to use oxygen and had the backing of a very strong Sherpa team.

The summit day was a long hard slog, but the pyramid itself suddenly gave some real climbing, scrambling over broken rock, scrabbling up snow-covered ice. I forgot my fatigue and became immersed in the climbing and then suddenly we were on top, the mountain falling away on every side, my first unclimbed peak and to this day the highest unclimbed peak I have ever attained. Great evil clouds were building up to the south and west. The monsoon was on the way; we had only just achieved success in time.

But though that success was all important to me, my richest memory of that expedition was walking out with just Tashi, the oldest of our Sherpas, over the Tilitso Pass, first discovered by Maurice Herzog in his 1950 recce, and enjoying three days of quiet companionship with this immensely wise and compassionate Sherpa.

In the Himalaya it is important to know how to pace yourself, how to contribute your fair share of work without burning yourself out. It is difficult getting the balance right, particularly on a siege-style expedition, which becomes a long struggle of attrition in which the climbers who do the most work could easily end up prejudicing their own chances of reaching the top. On the other hand, if everyone saves themselves, nobody gets to the top. In this respect an expedition that has a clear structure and leadership works much more smoothly, since a leader like Jimmy Roberts ensures that everyone has sufficient rest.

On a less structured venture, like the expedition to Nuptse (25,850ft/7879m) the following year, it is very much up to the individual. Some undoubtedly nursed themselves. Others, I in particular, hogged the lead and in the process risked burning myself out. At this stage I had very little understanding of the debilitating long-term effects of staying at altitude.

We made it to the top but we had certainly stretched things to the very limit. On getting back to the top camp from our successful ascent, the only provisions left were a few tea bags.

It emphasised the tightrope every expedition walks between glorious success and disaster. On this occasion we were lucky with the weather; Les Brown was lucky, when he slipped, climbing unroped down the summit gully. On most of my expeditions since then, there has been at least one moment when someone has had a narrow escape. I suspect this is so on all expeditions to the greater ranges. In my case all too many expeditions were to be overshadowed by tragedy.

In Patagonia, just two years later, I escaped by a hair's breadth, whilst abseiling on the descent. On the Central Tower of Paine (8760ft/2670m) the savagery of the weather made up for the lack of altitude. Three of us, however, had climbed together extensively in the Alps so shared a strong bonding of purpose and understanding. This gave us a unity that had been lacking on Nuptse and made the expedition altogether more satisfying.

But looking back at my diaries of all three expeditions, there was an underlying dissatisfaction, not so much with my own physical performance – after all I reached the top of all three mountains – but with my approach to the climbs. My need to be out in front, and especially to reach the top, was so great that it prevented me getting the most out of the total experience.

But these three expeditions were to stand me in good stead when I returned to expeditioning after a gap of nine years. They provided a foundation on which to build, not just the techniques of leading and organisation, but finding a deeper and more profound enjoyment of the mountain environment and the people with whom I climbed.

On the Paine expedition, despite many vicissitudes, unity of purpose and good morale proved the key to success. To counter the atrocious weather we made a prefabricated box tent which the team (*l to r*: Ian Clough, Derek Walker, Don Whillans, Barrie Page, Vic Bray and John Streetly) then portered up to Advance Base Camp.

The Anglo/Indo/Nepali Combined Services Expedition of 1960 was very traditional and run on ordered military principles. The team of ten climbers and nine Sherpas had a strong hierarchical structure and was skilfully led by Colonel James (Jimmy) Roberts.

The climb, in common with many on the higher peaks at that time, was a long snow slog. Yet three teams had already failed on it, possibly intimidated by its length: the final section involved a long high-altitude traverse from the shoulder of Annapurna 4 to the pyramid of Annapurna 2. On a final successful push, Dick Grant, Ang Nyima and I reached the top using oxygen.

Stewart Ward and I accompanied the gear which went by sea. Here we pose at the docks in Aden with our ship, the SS *Cilicia*, in the background.

On the shoulder below Annapurna 4, with Annapurna 3 in the background. The steep rock ridge on the left was tackled alpine-style in 1981, showing the evolution of skill and approach over two decades.

Acclimatisation camp below Annapurna 2.

Dick Grant, using oxygen, skirting Annapurna 4 at the start of the traverse to Annapurna 2.

Ang Nyima 'puts out more flags' in a traditional summit pose.

The successful summit team: Grant, Ang Nyima and myself.

A colourful group-photo taken on the first day of the long trek from Kathmandu to Sola Khumbu (*left to right*): Jimmy Roberts (who joined us for a few days), Jim Lovelock, Trevor Jones, Simon Clark, John Streetly, Les Brown and Jim Swallow.

Tashi, our most experienced Sherpa, with his wife and daughter during the approach march.

NUPTSE, 1961

In contrast to the order of the Annapurna expedition the Nuptse party had a more ad hoc style – a bunch of individualistic climbers all determined to have their own way. The expedition leader, Joe Walmsley, allowed the climbers who were advancing the route to make the key decision. This led to arguments but somehow we held together as a team. We were lucky to have a cadre of six dedicated Sherpas, including Tashi who had been on Annapurna 2. He was over fifty, a grandfather, and yet one of the strongest members of the team. With such a small party, climbers and Sherpas shared the tasks of lead climbing and load carrying.

Sherpa farmers working the land at 12,000 ft.

Jim Swallow carrying out basic dentistry on a Sherpani porter.

Thyangboche Monastery, spiritual centre of the Sherpa community.

Buddhist monks performing a religious ceremony above Junbesi, the gateway to Sola Khumbu.

NUPTSE (continued)

Moving through Sherpa country was a delight. There were no trekkers and we saw only three other Europeans during our trip. The Sherpas were subsistence farmers growing barley and potatoes. They also raised yaks for carrying loads, for ploughing, for milk and for the butter which was used in lamps as well as rancid in tea – a villainous brew flavoured with salt.

The Sherpas' trade with Tibet ended with the Chinese occupation and their main source of cash income was portering for expeditions. There were no medical facilities or schooling in Sola Khumbu at this time.

The view of the Everest group from Thyangboche. Everest peeps above the wall of Nupste with Lhotse on the right.

Joe Walmsley and I playing chess at Base Camp.

NUPTSE (continued)

Nuptse was Everest's last unclimbed summit. With our small team, an approach up the Khumbu Ice-fall was too complex and the only feasible route was on the South Face. This was obviously going to be as difficult as any alpine climb but with all the problems of altitude added – the first time that such a face had been attempted in the Himalaya.

The South Face of Nuptse. The summit is the rock turret to the right of the snow gully leading to the skyline in the centre of the picture. We used the long ridge leading in from the right to gain safe access to the centre of the face.

I tackle an ice pitch above Camp 3.

(*left*) A rock step on the ridge below Camp 3.

The Everest group from Thyangboche.

(*left*) The ice ridge below Camp 4 and (*inset*) looking down the route in this sector which took the rocks below the fragile crest.

NUPTSE (continued)

We used all our fixed rope on the complex ice ridge and had to buy second-hand rope locally. The sun action had sculpted the ice into crazy flutings that took a long time to climb. Morale flagged. Two of the team went home. The rest argued but slowly gained height in a drawn out battle of attrition.

From Camp 4 we had this magnificent view to the west over Taweche and Taboche to the great peaks of the Rolwaling Himal.

Above Camp 4 a snowfield led across to the crucial rock band which involved hard mixed climbing (*right*) to gain access to the upper snowfield.

Ang Pemba and I hacking out a platform for another tent at Camp 6.

Les Brown on the upper snowfield during the repeat climb.

Tashi leading up into the summit gully.

NUPTSE (continued)

We were at last working well as a team. Les Brown and I helped Dennis Davis and Tashi move up to make their ascent and then, with Jim Swallow and Ang Pemba, we repeated the climb next day.

The magnificent view of the South-West Face of Everest from the summit of Nuptse. As I gazed across the Western Cwm I little suspected that fourteen years later I would be leading the expedition making the first ascent of this huge face.

Expedition members after the climb (*left to right*) Les Brown, Jim Lovelock, Jim Swallow, myself, Trevor Jones, Joe Walmsley, porter, Tashi and Dennis Davis.

CENTRAL TOWER OF PAINE, 1962/3

The 1952 French ascent of Fitz Roy in the Patagonian Andes had drawn attention to this fabulous area of rocky spires. The Fitz Roy group captured the early limelight but Barrie Page's 1961 expedition to the Paine area of southern Chile returned with news of more splendid peaks. The Central Tower was the obvious challenge, and though only 8760ft/2670m, it was sheer on all sides. There was only one possible weakness on the West Face but its difficulty would be exaggerated by the savage South Pacific winds that constantly lash the area. Page realised that he needed a stronger party for such a project and he therefore invited Don Whillans, John Streetly, Ian Clough and me to join him, Derek Walker and Vic Bray for a renewed attempt.

We set off on the long voyage to South America late in 1962. Barrie Page was accompanied by his wife Elaine and two-year-old son, so I, just married, decided to bring my wife Wendy on a five-month honeymoon. We sailed during the Cuban missile crisis, passing a hundred miles south of the Russian merchant fleet.

(*left*) An aerial view of the Towers of Paine, with the Central and North Towers in the foreground and the Fortress beyond on the right.

(*right*) Collage of a voyage (clockwise from top left:) The SS *Reina del Mar* at La Rochelle; quayside conference; climbing practice on deck; Bonington and Whillans sun themselves whilst a fellow passenger can hardly bear to look; wardroom revelries – but who is on the bridge? Whillans won first prize at the fancy dress ball.

Derek Walker ferrying a load up to our Advance Base below the mountain.

The imposing eastern side of the Towers of Paine. We eventually climbed the Central Tower by a route just beyond its sunlit right profile. The East Face was climbed in 1974 by a South African expedition.

The western aspect of the Towers of Paine with the Central Tower on the right and the North Tower to its left.

CENTRAL TOWER OF PAINE (continued)

We reached Base Camp in late November. The East Face was clearly too difficult so we ferried loads round to the western flank where a great glacis of scree led to the col between the North and Central Towers. A rocky pedestal buttressing the lower part of the Tower was climbed but then the winds struck and it became a drawn out battle just to stay anywhere near the mountain. Our tents were ripped to bits and we finally retreated back to the valley for Christmas.

(*left*) Vic Bray and Barrie Page at Advance Base Camp with the Fortress in the background.

Whillans at Base Camp contemplating our lack of progress.

Don Whillans suggesting to the Italians that they climb elsewhere.

Whillans and Bray building the box.

John Streetly leading on the lower rocks.

The box, proof against the worst winds, erected within striking distance of the Tower. Whillans and Clough admire their work before taking up residence.

CENTRAL TOWER OF PAINE
(continued)

The continuous high winds kept us penned into Base Camp but at the end of December we were jolted out of our lethargy when an Italian expedition arrived, also bound for the Central Tower. We had a race on our hands!

Don Whillans and Vic Bray found a solution to the problem of the weather by building a pre-fabricated box from timber and tarpaulin which we were able to erect at the foot of the Tower. It was the precursor of the box tents used on the big Himalayan walls of the seventies. The hut allowed us to sit out the bad weather and move the route forward (using sisal fixed ropes) during the brief spells of calm weather. Eventually, during two fine days, Don and I made a bid for the summit. We had some narrow escapes. One of the fixed ropes, frayed by the wind, parted in Don's hands while he was leading. Somehow he maintained his balance, kept hold of both ends of the rope, retied them and continued! I had a short fall on the overhang, but continued up the steep granite groove, revelling in the feel of the sun-warmed rock.

Two views of John Streetly climbing the lower slabs heading towards the dièdre that provided the key to the climb.

Climbing the overhang in the dièdre, just after my short fall.

A view of the Towers from the box. The route went easily up to the col and then took the slab apron to gain the dièdre just right of the skyline.

Don and I resting at the col on the descent, just after my near demise, shaken after the fall.

CENTRAL TOWER OF PAINE (continued)

It was good to be climbing with Don again, leading alternate pitches on steep, technically difficult rock, anticipating each other's decisions and actions. We reached the summit at dusk and bivouacked just below the top. Next morning on the descent we passed the Italians climbing the dièdre. On the last abseil, the sisal rope parted and I fell 15ft only stopping myself on the brink

The dièdre above the overhang.

On the steep rock of the upper section.

Don in a victory pose on the summit.

Wendy and I reunited at Base Camp after my narrow escape.

of a 500ft drop. Our success had so nearly ended in disaster. Badly shaken, with a sprained ankle, I left the expedition, to explore southern Chile with Wendy.

4 *Adventure Journalist*

The Eiger Direct was my first professional assignment as a photographer. I had been asked because none of the regular *Daily Telegraph* photographers could climb to the positions needed. Half-way up the face, in a very cold snow cave, I was offered my next job in a radio message. The editor wanted me to go to Ecuador with a writer to photograph a story about Sangay, the most active volcano in the world. I immediately accepted. It was also the professional recognition I had been hoping for. Ever since starting to make a precarious living around my only skill, climbing, I had felt very vulnerable. For four years I had been lecturing about the North Wall of the Eiger and my expedition to Patagonia and writing my first book, *I Chose to Climb*. I had also been trying to improve my skills as a photographer, buying a single-lens reflex camera system and learning to develop and print black and white pictures.

The trip to Sangay was, in many ways, similar to a small mountaineering expedition. We were even going to climb a mountain. We needed to reach the top of the volcano but I also had to think of the kind of pictures I needed to tell the story economically in a few magazine spreads. Lecturing trains you to tell a picture story, but magazine photography is a much tighter discipline. I met Sebastian Snow, my first journalistic partner, at Quaglinos, an up-market restaurant in London. Sporting an Old Etonian tie, he was undoubtedly eccentric, probably neurotic, and enjoyed making outrageous statements, simply to watch the effect on his audience. Yet once out in Ecuador, we worked well together. He had plenty of contacts, quickly organised everything we needed to reach the foot of the volcano, kept going with dogged determination and did what he was told when we got into my area of expertise, the mountaineering. He was even prepared to return to make a second ascent because on the first the mountain had been in thick cloud and we failed to get any pictures.

I meanwhile was learning about the problems of keeping cameras working in the jungle humidity and rain. To get the picture of Don Albino and Sebastian crossing the river, I plunged into it myself, got the camera soaked and ruined much of the film. I had constant problems with fogged lenses and returned to find complete rolls of films unusable.

The following year, in Baffin Island in winter, the temperatures in the interior were down to −40°F. By this time I had changed my first camera system for a combination of Leicas and Nikons. I had them winterised and they kept working

(*right*) Don Albino (guide) and Sebastian Snow crossing the Volcan river near Sangay in the jungles of Ecuador in 1966 — typical of the many adventurous situations that I encountered as a photo-journalist. In the course of four assignments apart from the ice and storm of the Eiger, I had to cross swollen rivers, fight off bandits, avoid crocodiles, spend nights in igloos and struggle for my life in a Nile rapid — a catalogue of hazards that would not look out of place in an Indiana Jones adventure movie. My climbing background proved invaluable as it had accustomed me to handling high risk, extreme fatigue and mental stress and at the end of each assignment I had to return with a good selection of publishable photographs.

Courtiers of the Mir of Hunza.

The Mir of Hunza (*inset*) and his palace.

Nicholas Monsarrat in Hunza.

throughout the assignment without any extra protection from the cold. The problem came when rewinding, for the film was so brittle it tended to snap. Eventually I discovered a remedy, putting the ice-cold camera inside my parka to warm it up before rewinding. Another problem came when trying to photograph interiors, for the camera would frost over when exposed to a warm humid atmosphere.

Sebastian had also come out to Baffin Island but was unaccustomed to extreme cold, got a badly frostbitten nose on our first excursion and was forced to return home. This meant that I had to write the story as well as take the photographs. A similar thing happened later that year when I went to Hunza in the Karakoram with Nicholas Monsarrat, author of the great Second World War classic, *The Cruel Sea*. We were doing a story on the longevity of the people of Hunza, but the precarious jeep track had been swept away by landslide. Monsarrat was on a tight schedule so headed for home and, once again, I was left to complete all aspects of the story.

Up to this point I had been cast as the photographer. I was now credited with being able to write. I enjoyed being a photo-journalist in the fullest sense, since it meant having complete control of the assignment and I could take more suitable pictures as I was forming the story in my mind. On the Blue Nile I joined a largely military expedition that was trying to make the first complete descent. I stored my cameras in a watertight ammunition box in the bottom of the boat and had a waterproof Nikonos camera round my neck. I came uncomfortably close to being a war reporter when we were attacked on our way down river, even firing off five rounds from my revolver at gun flashes in the dark. Because we escaped unharmed, it was a strangely exhilarating experience, very similar to an epic on a climb.

Photo-journalism took me to places I would never have otherwise visited and, through the discipline of telling a picture story, made me much more aware of people and their surroundings. Yet, in the end, I began to feel a voyeur of other people's adventures and I yearned to get back to serious climbing. When I returned to expedition climbing in the seventies I found my media experience helped me to make a much fuller pictorial coverage of any climb. In addition, through lecturing and writing, I was also learning how to communicate my experience to a much wider audience than the climbing world.

I have always felt that popularising climbing is in the interest of the sport, but I did get a certain amount of criticism, particularly at the beginning for there is a strong amateur tradition within climbing. Yet there was nothing really new in what I was doing. Whymper had popularised mountaineering in the nineteenth century with his classic book, *Scrambles Amongst the Alps*. Captain John Noel had filmed the 1922 and 1924 Everest expeditions and, on his return, lectured to huge audiences both in Britain and the States, while in the thirties Frank Smythe earned a living as a writer and photographer recording his climbs and travels in a way very similar to the one I was to adopt. My profile was perhaps higher, as I was often involved in the more pervasive medium of television, but the message I was trying to present was theirs, communicating, as truly as I could, the whole rich field of mountaineering experience.

Emperor Haile Selassie leading Coptic Christian celebrations in Addis Ababa – a colourful event I witnessed during the Blue Nile expedition.

The distinctive domed hats favoured by the Andean Indians on sale at a shop in Cuenca.

Sebastian adopting a Clint Eastwood-like pose on his mule in the village of Limon.

The gentleman explorer – Sebastian Snow, business-suited and briefcased – arrives in the Ecuadorian interior, eager for adventure.

SANGAY, 1966

Our expedition to Sangay (17,496ft/ 5323m) was my first assignment as an adventure photographer. Sebastian Snow, an Old Etonian and gentleman adventurer, had already made a descent of the Amazon from its headwaters in the Andes and had crossed the Amazon basin from north to south. Now he wanted to climb Sangay in eastern Ecuador, reputed to be the most active volcano in the world. Although it had had several ascents, claiming at least one victim, it had never been climbed from the east, the side overlooking the jungle of the Amazon basin. Just getting to the foot of the volcano was an adventure. The maps were unreliable and much of the journey was through rain forest, at first on mules and then by foot. We stayed in the huts of the Jivaro Indians and as we neared the flanks of the volcano had to cut our way through the dense undergrowth and ford dangerously swollen rivers.

Inside a Jivaro hut: the slatted walls are designed for coolness and light.

(left) Crossing a jungle stream.

Hacking through jungle on the flanks of Sangay.

We had to pass through thirty miles of tropical rain forest to reach the eastern side of Sangay.

Indians crossing a river near Sangay.

The violent Volcan river, swollen with floodwater, formed a major obstacle in our path.

Sangay, immediately after a periodic eruption. It had an average of one every twenty-four hours but has been known to erupt 400 times in a day.

On the upper screes of the volcano the ground trembled beneath our feet, constantly threatening an eruption.

SANGAY (continued)

It was easy climbing but serious as we were a long way from help if anything had gone wrong and under constant threat of a major eruption. Lava bombs came bounding down the slope towards us and there was the occasional rumble beneath our feet. As we approached the top there was a pungent smell of sulphur. I waited by the crater for half an hour, half hoping to get a dramatic picture of an eruption at close quarters, but fearful of my chances of survival it if occurred.

Old and new: a skiddoo about to overtake our dog teams.

Constructing an igloo – once inside, with the stove going, it was warm and cosy.

An igloo at night.

The relaxed social life inside an Eskimo tent, lit and heated by a seal-oil lamp that doubled as a cooker.

BAFFIN ISLAND, 1967

I went to Pangnirtung, Baffin Island in February to record the way of life of the modern Eskimo. The days were short and the sun never came more than a few degrees above the southern horizon. Temperatures dropped as low as −40°F. Motorised skiddoos had become popular and there were only eight dog teams left to the few Eskimos who still went hunting for caribou and seal in the traditional way. I joined them on one of these hunting expeditions.

An Eskimo hunter shooting seal on the flow edge and then (*inset*) loading carcases into an igloo to be collected later.

Passing a beached iceberg in Cumberland Sound on the journey back to Pangnirtung.

BAFFIN ISLAND (continued)

We travelled for ten days by dog team, building igloo shelters each night, hunting first for caribou, without success, then going down to the flow edge to shoot seal. At their home base in Pangnirtung the Eskimos' double-layer tents, that had replaced the traditional skin tents since the arrival of the Hudson Bay Company, were now giving way to subsidised prefabricated houses with electricity and running water. The effects of modernisation were not entirely happy, with the majority living on welfare and a serious problem of alcoholism.

The upper reaches of the Blue Nile plunge through a series of gorges for 500 miles from the source on Lake Tana to the Sudanese frontier. The river had never been descended in full, although there had been five attempts between 1902 and 1965, one of which was stopped by a crocodile attack and another disrupted by an ambush in which two people were killed.

Captain John Blashford-Snell's military expedition, which I joined as the *Daily Telegraph* correspondent, had a curious period quality. We were armed and ready for attack and as the saga unfolded it began to resemble a Saturday-morning episode of *Sanders of the River*.

We avoided the Tisisat Falls just below Lake Tana.

(*left*) The Blue Nile gorge carving its way through the central Ethiopian plateau. (*inset*) Captain John Blashford-Snell, our leader.

The area of the upper Nile is inhabited by the fiercely independent Amharic tribesmen, Coptic Christians, most of whom are armed with rifles dating from the Ethiopian/Italian war.

Villagers watch us from Bahir Dar bridge where the Nile leaves Lake Tana.

(*left*) Launching our rubber dinghies.

Shooting the rapids of the first major cataract, a not altogether successful exercise.

BLUE NILE (continued)

We used three-man rubber dinghies for the first 150 miles of the river which had never been descended. It was soon clear that we had almost no control once we entered the rapids. We were frequently thrown out of the boats and I was nearly drowned in a big stopper wave. This was so dangerous that we opted to pull the boats through shallows to avoid the cataracts and at one point made a long portage through the jungle. During this manoeuvre Ian Macleod, my fellow crew member, was swept away and drowned when he attempted to swim a deep and swollen tributary stream to set up a rope bridge for the rest of the team.

Working the boats through flooded, overgrown and crocodile occupied channels and down little rapids (below) to avoid the main cataracts.

The rapids had been bad enough, but we were now going into even greater danger. We were attacked on two separate occasions by tribesmen living near the banks of the river. The first was an ambush which we escaped by paddling through a hail of stones and erratic gunfire and the second was a night attack on our campsite. Only the vigilance of our sentry saved us from massacre and we just managed to repel the attack. It all had the feeling of a *Boys' Own Paper* story, and yet was more dangerous than any climbing expedition I have undertaken.

The river opened out below the Portuguese bridge, some fifty miles from the source, but the gorge deepened and there were more crocodiles – Nile crocodiles are amongst the largest in the world.

Our flotilla on the lower stretches of the gorge in which we used four big assault boats.

Tribesmen at the Portuguese bridge. Some of these might have been amongst our attackers the following day.

The site of an ambush, when we were fired upon from the opposite bluff.

Blashford-Snell firing during our escape from the ambush.

(right) Alastair Newman, a territorial SAS captain, ready for more action.

Flags flying on the last lap of the river. Blashers should have been born in the days of Empire and punitive expeditions.

5 Himalayan Big Walls

By 1970 all the peaks of that magic height of 8000 metres had been climbed and most of the higher seven-thousanders. In this Golden Age of Himalayan climbing the principal objective was to make first ascents by the easiest route. These tended to be long snow plods, though there were exceptions such as Gasherbrum 4, Nuptse and K2, second highest mountain in the world, and certainly one of the most serious. In the late sixties political tension closed the Himalayan countries to foreign climbers. Kampa Tibetan rebels used bases in India and Nepal against the Chinese, and the struggle in Kashmir militarised the Indian/Pakistan border. It was as if a dam built in that period broke when the Himalaya was reopened in late 1969 and there was a flood of expeditions, the most powerful of which had their sights set on the big walls. The Japanese were quickly off the mark in the autumn of 1969 with a strong reconnaissance of the South-West Face of Everest, reaching the foot of the Rock Band at 27,000 ft. The following year our British team climbed the South Face of Annapurna, the Japanese made an even stronger bid on the South-West Face of Everest, Dr Herrligkoffer's German team, which included Reinhold Messner, climbed the Rupal Face of Nanga Parbat and the French established a beautiful route up the West Buttress of Makalu.

After three years of adventure journalism I was itching to go on another climbing expedition and when I saw a photograph of the South Face of Annapurna it caught my imagination. It seemed big and exciting and, without a thought for the logistical and climbing problems, I decided to go for it.

I had never really envisaged myself as the organising type and had a reputation for being absent-minded. It took some time for the scale of the challenge and the complexity of the necessary organisation to dawn on me. In the following months I was attacked by agonising moments of doubt. What if we arrived at the foot of the climb and decided it was unjustifiably dangerous and had to come home without even setting foot on the mountain?

The Mount Everest Foundation underwrote the cost of it, we were to be accompanied by a film crew, Don Whillans designed the box tents, successors to the Patagonian prefabricated hut, and also a waist harness, from which all subsequent harnesses have been developed. Mike Thompson put together our food and I did my best to co-ordinate it all. I was learning on the job and made plenty of mistakes, both whilst organising the expedition and subsequently on

Ian Clough traversing the fixed ropes on the steepest part of the Ice Ridge on our route on the South Face of Annapurna in 1970. This superb wall of rock and ice epitomises the challenge of big-wall climbing in the Himalaya, combining alpine-type difficulties with far greater scale and altitude. The various spurs have a cleanness of line that makes their ascent all the more satisfying. Our route up the Left-Hand Spur employed conventional tactics involving fixed ropes and a series of camps, but the subsequent Polish and Spanish ascents of the other obvious lines on the face were made in alpine or semi-alpine style.

the mountain itself. In many ways the South Face of Annapurna was the greatest challenge that I have ever faced and the most satisfying climb, since it was such a step into the unknown, into the realms of expedition leadership on a mountain face that was bigger and steeper than anything that had previously been attempted.

Our subsequent ascent of the South-West Face of Everest was a logical progression from what had been happening in the Alps on routes like the Eiger Direct, and indeed had been first mooted to me back in 1966 by John Harlin who, had he lived, would surely have been among the first contenders. In the early seventies the only possible method of climbing these huge faces seemed to be siege tactics which, in turn, meant a complicated expedition. I had learned the importance of sound organisation and effective delegation on Annapurna where I had tried to do too much myself. On Everest the team selection reflected these organisational necessities. It all came together particularly well in 1975. Hamish MacInnes, one of my oldest friends and deputy leader, was in charge of designing all our tentage, Dave Clarke, who ran an outdoors shop, got together the equipment and Mike Thompson organised the food. I gave them clear briefs and then left them to get on with it. I even used a computer to help plan the various flow alternatives of climbers, Sherpas and supplies between camps on the mountain. It meant that I retained a clear picture of my options once I was half-way up the face, with a mind starved of oxygen and addled by exhaustion. On the climb itself I tried to keep a close check on the general flow of the expedition, but once a group was briefed to go out in front, they took their own tactical decisions. Working with Pertemba, the sirdar of the Sherpas, I briefed him on the general strategy which he then carried out, carefully selecting the Sherpas for the various tasks.

On Everest in 1975 there were ten climbers with realistic summit aspirations. I felt I needed this number after experiencing the effects of attrition in our 1972 attempt, but there were problems in keeping them occupied. Only one pair could be out in front at a time doing the interesting work of making the route up the mountain. Inevitably there were some grumbles, but the teamwork was good and there was a dynamism within the expedition that helped everyone feel we had a real chance of success. With such a strong team it was very important to work from a basis of consensus while avoiding running it by committee. Having consulted and listened, I made my plans and then, where possible, called a meeting and asked for comments, only reserving the right of final decision to myself.

My effectiveness as leader was helped by the fact that I

Expedition stores arriving at Everest Base Camp in August, 1975.

Sherpas carrying crucial loads to Camp 5 on the South-West Face of Everest prior to the summit bid in October, 1975.

was climbing at around the same standard as my peers. It is hard for a leader to run an expedition from Base Camp. This was demonstrated in 1971 during the International Everest expedition, led by Norman Dyhrenfurth and Jimmy Roberts, and also on the 1972 Herrligkoffer expedition. I probably erred to the other extreme, finding excuses to get out in front making the route. But, once there, you tend to think emotionally and lose touch with what is happening to the rest of the expedition. The best position for the leader of a large expedition is at the camp immediately below that of the lead climbers. Here he can keep in touch with what is going on at the front and have a good feel for how the supplies are flowing up the mountain. This was the position adopted by John Hunt at the crucial stages of the 1953 Everest expedition and it still seems a sound one on more technical climbs.

Although we had been successful on Annapurna and Everest, we paid a terrible price for that success. On all four of my sieges on 8000-metre peaks, and then again in 1982, members of the team lost their lives. It's a frightening statistic. Were we reckless or just unlucky? I have spent much time agonising over this question for these were some of my closest friends and I have had to witness the cruelty of bereavement to their wives, girl friends, children and parents. I don't think it is a coincidence that all these accidents occurred on mountains of over 8000 metres, even though some of them happened on the lower slopes. There is something fundamentally more serious about the highest peaks. Their sheer size and scale mean that climbers have to pass danger points more frequently, the insidious effects of the lack of oxygen are infinitely more acute, and storms and avalanches are more ferocious. In such hazardous terrain there is a temptation to call the expedition off once the summit has been attained, so that the team can return successful and without any loss of life, but this would be a betrayal of the other members who worked so hard to put that first summit pair on top. Despite the prolonging of risk, they also deserve their chance of achieving their ambition.

Accidents fall into two very clear categories — those caused by objective dangers that could have entrapped anyone, and those where the climber takes a calculated risk. The former claimed the lives of Ian Clough, swept away by an ice avalanche on the glacier near the base of the South Face of Annapurna in the last minutes of the expedition, of Tony Tighe, in the Khumbu Ice-fall in 1972, and of Nick Estcourt who was killed by a huge windslab avalanche low on K2 in 1978. Mick Burke, on the other hand, took a calculated risk, which I suspect most of us would have taken, when he went for the summit of Everest alone in 1975. He almost certainly reached the summit but was overtaken by a storm and probably fell through the cornice on the way back. We don't know what happened to Peter Boardman and Joe Tasker when they set out to climb the unclimbed section of the North-East Ridge of Everest in 1982; they were undoubtedly pushing their own limits to the extreme, but this surely is one of the essential ingredients of climbing.

The very act of attempting a major peak over 8000 metres involves a high level of danger which, by careful planning and sober risk calculation, can be reduced to a degree, but it can never be eliminated, since absolute caution would stop you ever leaving Base Camp and would contradict the very point of our activity. I have to accept the fact that a high proportion of the expeditions I have led have had casualties. It's a burden that I do not bear lightly and yet it is one that I can accept, since the risks involved were something that the entire team accepted in their desire to achieve success on the mountain.

Our efforts on the Himalayan big walls brought out a very high level of teamwork and through that a greater understanding of each other. Critics of the use of siege tactics and oxygen on these climbs have suggested they should be left for a later generation who might be capable of climbing them in a purer style, but I believe climbing is an evolutionary process and the development of siege tactics on routes like Annapurna and Everest was part of a continuous progression that led to greater refinement and eventually bold alpine-style ascents, but the risks are high. In autumn 1988 four of Czechoslovakia's best climbers made the second ascent of the South-West Face, climbing alpine-style without oxygen. They had three bivouacs above 8200 metres, one of the team reached the summit, but they were all beginning to suffer from hallucinations and extreme exhaustion and they perished on the way back down to the South Col. This is a salutary reminder of the high element of risk in going for the summit of Everest without oxygen by any route. Technically difficult climbing at great altitude, which involves slow movement and bivouacs at over 8000 metres, has a particularly high risk level. I feel, therefore, that there is room for both the large siege expedition and the small alpine-style push. It is up to the climbers themselves to decide the method that is most suited to their own ability and the nature of the route they have selected.

ANNAPURNA SOUTH FACE, 1970

We started from Pokhara in March for a seven-day approach march into the Annapurna Sanctuary. The way took us through Tamang and Gurung regions, on a route that is now one of the most popular treks in Nepal. In 1970 very few people had penetrated the steep gorge of the Modi Khola and we saw no other Europeans on our way to the mountain.

Children group around scarce books in the village school at Chandrakot.

Gurung girls in the village of Ghandrung.

Our 140-strong well-disciplined porter train.

All available land is terraced to cultivate rice or barley.

From our Base Camp in a snow-covered meadow at 14,000ft we had our first full view of the daunting 10,000ft wall of steep ice and rock we had come to climb. The summit of Annapurna (26,545ft/ 8091m) was at the top of the Left-Hand Spur which was our chosen route. An obvious ice ridge led up to mid-height snow slopes, above which the way was barred by a prominent rock band which we assumed would be the crux. Nothing of this standard had ever been attempted in the Himalaya. My closest experience was on Nuptse but this face was both larger and steeper. I estimated that the Ice Ridge would take us three days to climb but in the event it took eighteen, with climbers taking turns at the exhausting business of advancing the route over the tortuous ice bosses and cornices (*right*).

The box tent (*left*) was developed by Don Whillans from the concept we had used in Patagonia in 1963. Built with a strong frame of alloy tubing, it was to prove an effective tool for steep face climbing, usable on small ledges and capable of withstanding a build up of snow that would have crushed a conventional tent.

(*left*) Don Whillans and Mick Burke at Base Camp with the South Face of Annapurna in the background.

(*right*) Martin Boysen approaching one of the steepest sections of the Ice Ridge. On the Rock Band towering above we were luckily able to change our planned route up the obvious dièdre in favour of an easier route up the left flank.

Dougal Haston on the fixed ropes on the Ice Ridge above Camp 4

Leaving Camp 5 (22,750ft) to tackle the Rock Band.

(*right*) Don Whillans moving up from Camp 3 with dexion stakes to anchor the fixed ropes. Machapuchare dominates the background scene.

(*above, left and below*) Mick Burke in action on the Rock Band which he and Tom Frost climbed after several days of sustained effort, thereby opening the route to the summit.

ANNAPURNA SOUTH FACE
(continued)

Our two big-wall experts, Mick Burke and Tom Frost, forced the steep part of the Rock Band to establish Camp 6 at 24,000ft. This involved what was probably the most difficult rock and mixed climbing to have been done at that altitude. Don Whillans and Dougal Haston then moved up to the high camp, fixing rope up a snow gully leading to the crest of the Rock Band. Then they sat out a week of bad weather, sustained by a trickle of supplies carried up by the now exhausted team. When the weather improved they gained the summit with an impressive one-day climb, climbing unroped for most of the way, reaching the top (*right*) just as the weather began to worsen.

Don Whillans on the summit (a 16mm movie frame).

(*below*) Expedition members at the end of the climb. The original party of eleven climbers, backed by six Sherpas, proved unable to sustain a prolonged siege, and we recruited some trekkers, 'the London Sherpas', to assist us. Our numbers were further swelled by the television team that covered the climb.

Climbing team: 1 Tom Frost, 2 Chris Bonington, 3 Kelvin Kent (Base Camp Manager), 4 Dougal Haston, 5 Mike Thompson, 6 Don Whillans, 7 Nick Estcourt, 8 Mick Burke, 9 Martin Boysen, 10 Dr David Lambert; **Sherpas and other porters**: 11 Tukte, 12 Ang Pema, 13 Gumbahadur Pun, 14 Pasang Kami, 15 Pembatharke, 16 Sonam Tenzing, 17 Nima Tsering, 18 Mingma Tsering, 19 Kancha; **T.V. Team**: 20 John Soldini, 21 Jon Lane, 22 John Edwards, 23 Alan Hankinson; **London Sherpas and others**: 24 Frank Jackson, 25 Robin Terray, 26 Unknown, 27 Cynthia Gilbey, 28 Barbara Jackson

Ian Clough and myself in the Whillans Box at Camp 4.

Below the ice wall on the glacier above Camp 1 where Ian Clough was engulfed by the avalanche.

Ian's funeral on the hill above Base Camp. We carved an inscription on a nearby rock (*inset*).

The view to Annapurna 2 from the South Face of Annapurna 1.

ANNAPURNA SOUTH FACE (continued)

The expedition was very nearly at an end and the mountain had been cleared. Ian Clough and Mike Thompson were the last to come down, after supervising the Sherpas stripping some of the lower camps. On the descent below Camp 2 they were passing beneath séracs and ice walls – the last potentially dangerous place on the mountain – when one of the walls collapsed and swept down on them. Mike jumped back into the shelter of a small ice wall, but Ian tried to outrun the avalanche and was caught and swept to his death.

We recovered his body and buried it just above Base Camp. I had enjoyed some of my best climbing days with Ian on the Grandes Jorasses and the Eiger. He was a great partner and a wonderful expedition member, a selfless, easy-going, yet forceful climber, prepared to take on any task. It was Ian who had gone out to Bombay to accompany the expedition gear, delayed in its sea crossing. He had shepherded it through customs, then accompanied it on a lorry across India to Pokhara and, with the porters, all the way to Base Camp, while we had started on the route with the bare minimum of equipment.

We had succeeded on a major route against all the odds, faced by deteriorating weather and the growing fatigue of the team and then, in the euphoria of our success, our joy was destroyed by the loss of our friend in the last moments of the expedition.

The South-West Face of Everest.

The porters carried loads of around 25 kilos.

All the streams were in spate and many of the crossings were dangerous.

THE SOUTH-WEST FACE OF EVEREST, 1972

The huge face of Everest (29,028ft/ 8848m), towering over the Western Cwm was the great challenge of the early seventies. After the two Japanese attempts in 1969 and 1970, the heavily publicised International expedition was weakened by illness and arguments and a later Anglo-German bid also failed. The face appeared technically easier than the South Face of Annapurna but its principal problem was breaching the Rock Band that barred the face at a height of 27,000ft – higher than the summit of Annapurna. Overcoming this high obstacle at the end of a long and tenuous supply line proved a more complex problem than expected. It was as much the difficulty of maintaining a flow of supplies up to the base of the Rock Band as the difficulty of the Band itself that had stopped the earlier attempts.

In 1972, with a unified expedition combining several climbers who had been on Annapurna and Everest, we felt we had a better chance of success than our predecessors. But we could only mount the attempt in the post-monsoon season which meant colder conditions on the mountain and completing the approach march during the torrential rains of the monsoon, with leeches reaching out from almost every leaf. The benefits were the lush green of the grass and the abundance of wild flowers along the way.

Porters passing through the Sherpa hamlet of Julming in the Dudh Kosi valley south of Namche Bazar.

After our damp approach march we congregated in Sola Khumbu to organise and equip our twenty-four Sherpas. The development of trekking and climbing had boosted the local economy and by Nepalese standards the Sherpas were well paid. One of the most desirable expedition perks was the gear allocation – important not only for their comfort and safety on the climb but also for its resale value. After this we moved up to establish our Base Camp in mid-September.

Bedraggled team members shelter from the rain for a few minutes at the tea house in Takshindu:
(*left to right*) Nick Estcourt, Dave Bathgate, Kelvin Kent, Dougal Haston, Graham Tiso and Hamish MacInnes.

The porters sheltering under their polythene sheets.

Everest towering above the Khumbu Glacier. We established our Base Camp below the Ice-fall on the left.

Graham Tiso and Dougal Haston issuing gear to our Sherpas.

A view up the 2000ft Khumbu Ice-fall with tiny figures in the centre of the picture showing its massive scale. The summit of Nuptse is the highest point on the right retaining wall. The steep sérac walls at the top of the Ice-fall required ladders to make a reasonable route for laden Sherpas (*inset*).

Oxygen cylinders stockpiled at Camp 1.   Sherpa porters setting out from Camp 1.

THE SOUTH-WEST FACE
OF EVEREST (continued)

In the fine autumn weather we made fast progress up the Ice-fall. To assist the easy passage of supplies we laddered walls and crevasses and fixed ropes in any awkward places. With Sherpas carrying loads up it on a daily basis, constant maintenance work was needed to repair the damage caused by the continual glacial movement.

Just above Camp 1 there is a full view of the Western Cwm, one of the highest and most beautiful mountain prospects in the world. Many expeditions have passed this way since 1952 including the one making the first ascent by the line up across the Lhotse Face to the South Col at the end of the Cwm. The route up the Cwm makes great transverse detours to turn huge crevasses (*inset*) that span the glacier at various points and eventually leads to the site of Camp 2 — the traditional Advance Base Camp for all expeditions using this approach. Marker flags are essential to avoid losing the path in poor visibility.

Graham Tiso is treated by Barney Rosedale after being hit by a stone at Camp 4.

Camp 2 (Advance Base) with the South-West Face in the background. Camp 3 (23,000ft) was placed under a rock buttress at the top of the initial ice-field on the right and Camp 4 in the centre of the face near the top left corner of the picture.

Doug Scott making repairs to Camp 4, devastated during the big storm.

Dr Barney Rosedale cooking at Camp 2 where, even during the day, it was often very cold.

THE SOUTH-WEST FACE OF EVEREST (continued)

With the weather remaining calm we advanced the route up the face to establish Camp 4 at 24,600ft by October 12. But then the winds hit us and it became a struggle just to remain on the face, let alone make any progress. The jet stream had shifted in height and direction to bring the upper slopes of Everest into its full blast, wearing down the team in a savage process of attrition.

After a severe storm at the end of October, there was a calm spell during which we managed to establish Camp 5 below the Rock Band. The next ten days were spent trying to establish Camp 6 at the right end of the Rock Band.

The weather conditions were now gruelling. The skies were cloudless but the temperatures were down to −40°F and with winds up to 90mph. It was difficult to keep warm, even in a full down suit inside one's sleeping bag, and Camp 5, shaded from the morning sun, was like a deep freeze.

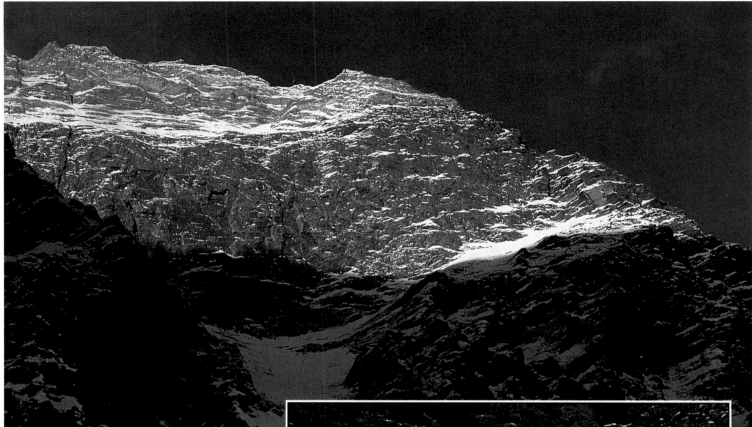

Sunset came early in November with icy shadows moving up the face forcing us into camp and our sleeping bags.

Mick Burke erecting a box tent at Camp 5 – the coldest camp I have ever experienced.

(*right*) We took turns at pushing the route forward above Camp 5, moving up to the right end of the Rock Band.

While we worked the route across below the Rock Band we began to wonder whether the gully breaching its left end (in the top left corner of the photograph) might not offer a better route.

Dougal Haston at the site for Camp 6.

The gully in the Rock Band, devoid of snow.

THE SOUTH-WEST FACE OF EVEREST (continued)

The final bid to establish Camp 6 on November 14 was frustrated by high winds and, in addition, we found that the gully through the Rock Band, that Haston and Whillans had tried in 1971 (during the International expedition), was swept clean of snow and far too difficult in the conditions. We were thus forced to call off the attempt. Yet we didn't feel dispirited, for we had taken ourselves to the limit in the harshest conditions and in the process learned much that would be invaluable in another attempt.

In a horrifying replay of the Annapurna tragedy, Tony Tighe was killed in the Ice-fall. Tony had been helping in Base Camp and to reward him I agreed to him accompanying Sherpas on a trip to Camp 1 to bring down the final loads, so that he should enjoy the wonderful view up the Western Cwm. Moving a little more slowly than the Sherpas, he was caught when an ice-tower collapsed. It could have happened to any one of us – such is the cruel Russian roulette of the Khumbu Ice-fall where it is impossible to guarantee a safe route.

Sherpas hurrying down the Ice-fall where the route passed below the ice-tower.

Looking up to where the tower collapsed to bury Tony Tighe.

Tony Tighe, our good humoured Australian helper.

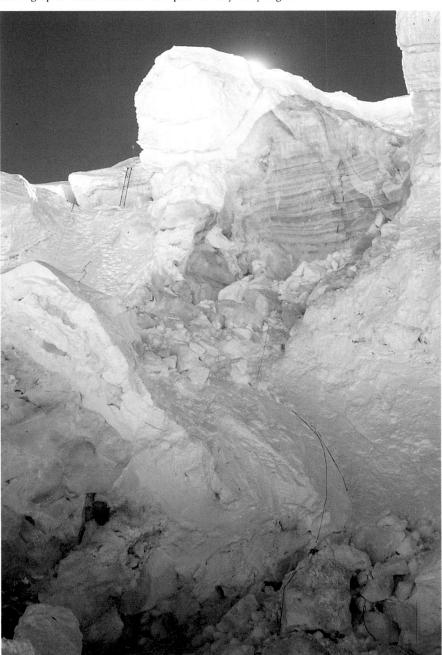

Hamish MacInnes and the Ice-fall Sherpas searched the debris but found nothing.

THE SOUTH-WEST FACE
OF EVEREST (continued)

I led another attempt in the
post-monsoon season of
1975. This time nothing was
left to chance, much of the
planning was done on
computer and we refined our
equipment, particularly the
tentage and oxygen gear. I
assembled a very strong team
with eighteen climbers and
eighty high-altitude Sherpas.
We started earlier than in

1972, having flown our
equipment to Lukla before
the monsoon from where it
was transported by yak and
porter and stored in a barn in
Khumde until our arrival.
This was managed entirely
by our Sherpas led by
Pertemba, the sirdar. He
was the youngest Sherpa
ever to be given this
responsibility and he proved
to be an excellent leader
and a first class
administrator.

Organising the kit issue.

Pertemba, our able sirdar.

Sound logistics were the key to our success: working out the flow of
supplies up the mountain.

Our organisation camp next to our expedition 'warehouse' at Khumde.

Porters ferry loads up the ice-field towards Camp 3, set in the shelter of the rocks above. Camp 4 (*right*) was in a more exposed site where Hamish MacInnes's improved design of box tent was particularly useful.

THE SOUTH-WEST FACE OF EVEREST (continued)

We established Base Camp in late August, a month earlier than in 1972, and two weeks later we were at work on the face itself. We had begun the climb before the end of the monsoon and it snowed every day, so we had to watch out for avalanches. But it was a race against the arrival of the winter winds and biting cold that had defeated us in 1972. The lead climbers were split into three teams with some of the best Sherpas to help them to advance the route quickly, establishing the camps and fixing the ropes for the porters ferrying supplies behind them. We started using oxygen for sleeping at Camp 4.

Ronnie Richards crossing the upper part of the Central Couloir with Camp 5, sheltered from the threat of avalanche in a small gully, in the background.

THE SOUTH-WEST FACE OF EVEREST (continued)

On September 16 Ronnie Richards and I established Camp 5 at 25,500ft. I made this my command post for the rest of the expedition. The crucial phase of the attack on the Rock Band by the Left-Hand Gully was to follow and I wanted to get a feel for the nature of the terrain and how the supplies were flowing.

We were in a strong position being well ahead of the winter winds, with plenty of reserves of manpower, both for forcing the route and maintaining the flow of supplies up the mountain.

Tarpaulins gave extra avalanche protection to Camp 4.

A powder-snow avalanche cascading down the Left-Hand Gully through the Rock Band.

Mick Burke on the fixed ropes in the gully. The key section at the top was up a steep snow-plastered ramp (*inset*) which led up to the site of Camp 6.

THE SOUTH-WEST FACE OF EVEREST (continued)

Dougal Haston and Doug Scott at Camp 6, with Mike Thompson, who carried one of the vital loads, in the background.

On September 20 Nick Estcourt and Paul ('Tut') Braithwaite climbed the gully through the Rock Band. They ran out of oxygen, but kept going, with Nick leading a difficult mixed pitch. With the way open we established Camp 6 at 27,300ft two days later, with Doug Scott and Dougal Haston in residence poised for a summit bid. We had timed it right. The monsoon clouds were still over Nepal but we were above them. There was little wind and it was comparatively warm at −10°C. This was my high point on the face. I had taken part in the carry in support of the summit pair. Now it was up to them.

Dougal Haston on the final steps to the summit at dusk.

Haston on the summit, suffused with happiness in the last rays of sunlight.

Doug Scott celebrates a safe return to Camp 6 after a cold night in a snow hole.

Pete Boardman's photograph of the final sweep of the South-East Ridge from the gully below the South Summit. Scott's and Haston's tracks along the ridge are clearly visible, as is the Hillary Step in the centre of the picture.

Mick Burke – last seen just below the summit.

THE SOUTH-WEST FACE OF EVEREST (continued)

Scott and Haston fixed 1000ft of rope across the summit snow field and made their bid for the top the following day, completing the ascent at 6pm. They bivouacked in a snow hole on their descent and worked all night massaging themselves to avoid frostbite. It was an outstanding climb, the climax of a fine team effort.

Two days later Pete Boardman, Pertemba, Mick Burke and Martin Boysen made their attempt. Boysen's oxygen failed and he turned back. Boardman and Pertemba reached the summit and met Burke on their descent. Burke continued upwards while they descended in worsening weather, waiting for him at the South Summit. He never returned and, with a blizzard blowing, they concluded he must have walked through a cornice in the white-out. Triumph had turned to bitter tragedy.

6 Small Teams, Fine Peaks

There's a special attraction in an unclimbed peak; the knowledge that no one has ever stood there before or has enjoyed that particular 360° view from the summit. There is also a simplicity of aim, to reach the top by the easiest possible route, that has a strength of its own. With the Chinese ascent of Shisha Pangma in 1964, all the peaks of over 8000 metres had been climbed, but there was still a host of 7000-metre peaks awaiting an ascent and literally hundreds of peaks over 6000 metres. Quite apart from the satisfaction of reaching virgin summits, you can actually enjoy yourself. Base Camps are lower, usually below the snow line, making it easier to recuperate in the relatively oxygen-rich atmosphere and to relax in a way that is always difficult in the constant glare of snow or on the rubble of a glacier moraine. It's possible to acclimatise to the point of climbing at almost alpine levels of movement up to 6000 metres. Above 8000 metres every step becomes a desperate effort.

The three trips portrayed in this chapter were sandwiched between much bigger expeditions to the great walls of Annapurna, Everest and K2. Each one was very different in character but had the common factor of being to particularly attractive unclimbed peaks. Brammah (21,030ft/6416m), the smallest, is a near perfect pyramid of snow and rock at the head of the Kiba Nullah in Kishtwar, Changabang (22,520ft/6864m) is a shark's tooth of grey granite on the perimeter wall of the Nanda Devi Sanctuary, and the Ogre, or Baintha Brakk (23,900ft/7285m) is a towering three-headed giant that peers over the outer wall of the Biafo Spires, above the Biafo Glacier.

They also covered widely differing terrain, people and cultures, from the forested valleys of Kishtwar, with their wooden Swiss peasant-style houses, to the windowless mud clad, flat-roofed villages, clinging above the arid gorges of the Braldu river. There was the beauty of the Nanda Devi Sanctuary, with the forbidding gateway of the Rishi Gorge, first penetrated by Eric Shipton and Bill Tilman, guarding cool forests and flower-covered upland pastures. There were different people, too; the Hindu villagers of Tappobam, just below the Rishi Gorge, the Gugars who take their flocks each summer from the plains to the high mountain valleys of Kishtwar, the Shi'ite Baltis of Askole at the head of the Braldu Gorge, excitable, argumentative yet warm-hearted and hospitable.

Our teams were smaller than the ones we needed for the big faces and there

The granite tooth of Changabang stands on the perimeter of the Nanda Devi Sanctuary and in 1974 was unclimbed. The peak had tantalised mountaineers for years but access was restricted throughout the sixties. It was an obvious challenge once the restrictions eased. The best line for the first ascent of an unclimbed peak is not always obvious in advance. We had hoped to tackle the mountain by its arresting North-West Ridge (*left*) but on inspection found that this was too hard. We therefore crossed Shipton's Col (the rock saddle on the right) to try a route up the snowy South Face.

was less pressure on organisation and funding, which meant less commitment to anyone other than ourselves. The expeditions to Brammah and Changabang were joint ventures with Indian climbers. At the time neither Kishtwar nor the Garhwal was open to foreigners and this was the only way to climb there. It meant climbing with people we didn't know well, who came from a very different cultural background from ourselves, which presented some minor problems on the mountain, but it certainly made the organisation easier, and brought us new friendships, which have lasted over the years. This was particularly the case with my co-leader on both expeditions, Balwant Sandhu, a colonel in the Paratroops. We had much in common through a shared military background, a love of climbing and an impatience with all forms of bureaucracy.

Each venture was close to being an alpine trip. On Brammah, the British contingent consisted of myself and Nick Estcourt, one of my closest friends. He was a talented and forceful climber who had managed to hold down a full time job as a computer programmer while going regularly on expeditions. My selection of the Changabang team in 1974 was once again based on friendship combined with climbing ability – Martin Boysen, a brilliant rock climber with whom I'd been climbing since the early sixties, Dougal Haston whom I had got to know well on the Eiger Direct, and Doug Scott who had been with me on Everest in 1972 and was beginning to emerge as one of Britain's most forceful mountaineers.

Whilst Brammah had felt very much like an alpine holiday, Changabang, with a team of four Indian climbers and four Britons, was more like a conventional expedition. The different cultures were very apparent when it came to the decision-making process. Balwant Sandhu had absolute authority over his Indian contingent. It was something both they and he expected. I, on the other hand, within our small British group, arrived at decisions through consultation. My role was that of a chairman of a committee. On the one occasion I took a unilateral decision and made a recce of our Base Camp site with Dougal Haston I brought down upon myself the ire of Balwant Sandhu, Doug and Martin, whom I had not consulted. I had to admit they were right. It was very different from the larger siege-style expedition in which the leader does need to make the decisions, although even here it is important that he is aware of the opinions of team members. On a small expedition leadership shifts from one climber to another depending upon circumstances. It is the person who is most fitted at any particular time, either through greater fitness, determination, or expertise at solving a specific problem, who takes the lead.

Doug Scott invited me to join his expedition to the Ogre shortly after we got back from Everest in 1975. It was to be a very different kind of undertaking. Not only was it to be a small team but the six climbers were to split into three pairs with each partnership choosing their own route and climbing it in whatever style appealed to them. At first things went well with three weeks of blue skies and sunshine. It led us, perhaps, to start taking the mountain for granted. Initially there was a level, not so much of competition, as of very different interpretations of the best way of going about the climb. However, after Tut Braithwaite had been injured by stonefall and Nick Estcourt and I had made our own abortive but very close attempt on the main peak, satisfying ourselves with the West Summit 300 metres or so lower than the Central one, we began to realise that we would have to work together as a single unit. The four of us who were still fit, Doug Scott, Mo Anthoine, Clive Rowland and I, made one final attempt.

The story of our ascent, Doug's accident and our subsequent retreat is told in the picture story. Crisis and the struggle for survival welded us into an effective, close-knit team. It was certainly the most harrowing experience that either Doug or I have ever had and yet throughout the long drawn out retreat there was never a sense of despair. This was largely due to the quality of the support we had from Mo and Clive, and the fact that none of us lost his will to survive or showed the doubts that we might secretly have held. Nonetheless it was a close run thing. We could never have carried Doug down the mountain; he had to crawl. I can think of very few people who would have had his stoicism or stamina. After I had fallen whilst abseiling and broken my ribs, I realised I had to get down quickly, for pneumonia was setting in, but we were trapped by a storm and could only move when there was sufficient visibility to cross the featureless col that led to the top of the fixed ropes. I curled up in my soaking wet sleeping bag, dried it out with my own meagre body heat and made myself

Climbing an ice ridge high on the Ogre with a magnificent south-easterly panorama of the Karakoram range behind me. "The attraction of tackling unclimbed peaks with small teams . . . is the sense of freedom, exploration and sheer fun . . . it engenders."

as comfortable as possible, holding firmly onto life. It was a matter of telling myself that however painful the moment was, this pain and discomfort were ephemeral; in a few days we'd be back at the bottom of the mountain lying on the sun-warmed grass of Base Camp and in a few weeks I'd be back home with Wendy. Rather than fighting the mountain to survive, it was necessary to accept the situation, almost becoming part of the mountain and then, attuned with the environment, we could extricate ourselves from a desperate situation. Individual will power and self-confidence are important, and so is unity within the team as a whole. It was this that enabled us to retreat safely.

The small team, provided that it is compatible, that each of its members is equally self-reliant and yet prepared to support the others if necessary, has a natural strength of its own. Its very isolation on mountains far from any external help increases the sense of self-sufficiency and makes the experience more profound. I shall never forget the moments after Doug abseiled from just below the summit of the Ogre. The light was fading fast and the mountains were dark silhouettes against a purple sky, K2 a distant pyramid, dominating the peaks around it. There was no wind, no sound, and I was alone in this magnificent firmament, at peace after the hectic race for the summit, loving what I saw, that sense of beauty enhanced by the very level of commitment we had made. And then the silence was shattered by Doug's thin scream as he slipped and penduled across the face. Yet the painful struggle for survival that followed has its own rich memories, its moments of humour and lessons to be learnt.

It is not coincidental that the fatalities I have experienced on expeditions have been on peaks of over 8000 metres. We certainly came close to death on the Ogre, but its slightly lower height gave us greater margin for error, a greater chance of survival with broken legs or ribs, and so we were able to find our way down. But the attraction of tackling unclimbed peaks with small teams is not in the greater safety factor. It is the sense of freedom, exploration and sheer fun, as well as challenge that it engenders. Certainly some of my best memories come from these expeditions.

Goats crossing a snow slope in the Rishi Gorge.

CHANGABANG, 1974

The Nanda Devi Sanctuary, surrounded by steep mountain walls, was first penetrated in 1934 by Eric Shipton and Bill Tilman. They forced a route through the precipitous Rishi Gorge and explored one of the most inaccessible and beautiful mountain cirques in the world. We also used the Gorge on our approach to Changabang.

(*right*) Members of the expedition: (back row) Kiran Kumar, Martin Boysen, Tashi Chewang, Doug Scott, Dougal Haston and Ujagar Singh; (front row) Chris Bonington, D. J. Singh, Balwant Sandhu.

Nanda Devi seen from the slopes of Changabang.

The four Britons, Balwant Sandhu and Tashi, made the first ascent of Changabang in a two-day climb up the South Face to gain the Changabang/ Kalanka Col and thence by the East Ridge. Throughout the climb we had increasingly fine views of Nanda Devi, first climbed in 1936 by Tilman and Noel Odell and an Anglo-American expedition. Balwant Sandhu was later to be co-leader of an Franco-Indian team that made the first traverse of the two peaks of the mountain.

(*right*) Approaching the col above which the East Ridge leads to the summit of Changabang.

Typical Kishtwar countryside.

A Gugar sage.

On the approach march.

A spectacular waterfall in the Kibar Nullah.

BRAMMAH, 1973

Kishtwar is an attractive mountain range with (in 1973) many unclimbed 6000 metre peaks. The area, which lends itself to alpine-style climbing, has become very popular in recent years. Nick Estcourt and I joined up with an Indian expedition to attempt Brammah (21,030ft/6416m), one of the most distinctive peaks of the range. An additional bonus is the approach through pine-forested valleys leading to the impressive Kibar Nullah, home of the semi-nomadic Muslim Gugar tribe.

(*left*) On the lower part of Brammah's South Ridge, looking across the Kishtwar range to Brammah 2.

(*right*) Englishmen abroad – Nick and I stop for tiffin at a tea shop during the approach march.

A Gugar woman spinning cotton.

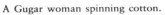

Erecting a makeshift bridge.

BRAMMAH (continued)

We established a high camp on the South Ridge and made one attempt with Ujagar Singh and Tashi but found we were not fully acclimatised and had to turn back. Nick and I then climbed the mountain in unsettled weather over two days. The route was similar to a straightforward alpine classic, situated in a magnificent setting of marvellous peaks. There was a nagging seriousness, however, for there was no rescue back-up and we were very much on our own.

Nick Estcourt tackling a steep section of the ridge at about 5600 metres.

Our camp on Brammah.

The South Ridge of Brammah rising from the left – the camp was on the shoulder at its base.

Nick pauses just below the summit at the beginning of the descent. In the background are Flat Top (left) and Pt. 20,039 (6107m) on the right.
I attempted this in 1976 with Ronnie Richards, getting about two-thirds of the way up the central spur.

The Skardu valley from the Braldu Gorge.

THE OGRE, 1977

In Baltistan on my first visit to the Karakoram I was struck by the contrast with Nepal, Garhwal and Kishtwar. It is a harsh land of deserts, rock and steep snow peaks, relieved by the occasional emerald jewels of terraced fields and orchards,

(*left*) Balti porters – volatile, argumentative but resourceful.

Terraced and irrigated fields around a village set on a high shelf above the Braldu. The irrigation ditches from the river show as strips of vegetation across the arid hillside above the village.

Porters on a section of pathway, built against a cliff in the Braldu Gorge and supported by stones and spars.

eked out of the landscape by irrigation from the turbid glacial waters. The people reflect the land. There is none of the humour of the Sherpas or the gentleness of the Nepalese. The Baltis are volatile and argumentative, with a hint of violence. Though resourceful in their agriculture, they have yet to tap the trading potential of the many expeditions that pass their villages. There is little relaxation on a Karakoram approach march.

The Ogre emerges from behind its wall of satellite peaks in this view from half-way up the Biafo Glacier.

THE OGRE, 1977

The Ogre, with its three summits and serried rock walls, presented a superb unclimbed challenge. Doug Scott's plan was for us to tackle it in pairs, each by a separate route. He partnered Tut Braithwaite to try the Central Spur. Mo Anthoine and Clive Rowland had the West Ridge and Nick Estcourt and I had designs on the South Face. This unstructured approach worked well with such a group of individualists and, as the expedition developed, we adjusted our plans according to circumstances.

Approaching the mountain: Scott and Braithwaite attempted the mist-wreathed buttress, the rest of us climbed the mixed face below the col.

(*below*) On the rock and snow rib leading to the col. We fixed ropes on this section which proved important in our subsequent desperate retreat.

The upper section of the Ogre from the col. The West Ridge is on the left. Nick Estcourt and I traversed the glacial terrace above the ice cliffs to turn the buttress on the right to gain access to the South Face.

From a snow hole at the bottom corner of the South Face, we launched our attempt, first climbing fixed ropes up difficult slabs (climbed a day earlier) to gain access to the ice face that led to the summit ridge.

THE OGRE (continued)

From the camp on the col Nick and I made our summit bid by the South Face. We took the glacier terrace and climbed a band of slabs to gain access to the face, then,

after a rest day in a snow hole, made a dash for the top, only to find when we gained the summit ridge that the rocky Central Summit was too difficult as we had brought little rock equipment. We settled for the first ascent of the West Summit, and retreated.

As we gained height on the South Face we were rewarded by magnificent views across the Latok group to Masherbrum (*above*) and K2 (*inset*).

Doug had joined Mo and Clive on the West Ridge. With Nick fatigued, I joined the West Ridge team and after a two-day climb we crossed the West Summit and bivouacked in a snow hole. Next day Doug and I tackled the summit tower. The climbing was difficult and strenuous, requiring pendulums to make progress. We reached the summit on a wonderfully clear and still evening. During the abseil descent, Doug slipped on verglas, pendulumed and broke both his legs in the impact. The climb now became a struggle for survival and, after a bivouac, we regained the snow hole to face the long descent.

The rock pillar at the base of the West Ridge which was climbed by Mo Anthoine and Clive Rowland and equipped with fixed ropes.

The last fixed ropes on the Pillar, at the point where I fell during the retreat.

Another rock step on the ridge was turned by this ice slope.

From the West Buttress we enjoyed views across the ranges north of the Hispar Glacier where Kanjut Sar is the dominant peak.

One of the difficult crack pitches on the summit tower. The South Face drops away steeply below with the sunlit glacier shelf, where Nick and I had our first snow hole, at the top left edge of the photo. (*inset*) Doug Scott on the summit at dusk.

Looking back from the summit tower to the West Summit. The tracks lead to the snow cave.

Clive and Mo in the snow cave.

Clive Rowland breaks out of the cave into the storm outside.

Doug preparing for the descent.

We were now in a desperate position and, to make matters worse, the weather broke, forcing us to remain in the snow hole for two days, eating the last of our food. On the third day, with the storm still raging, we forced our way back over the West Summit. Mo broke the trail and Doug was able to crawl behind, helped by Clive and me. We could never have carried him. After another bivouac we began the descent of the Pillar where, on the first abseil, I fell, breaking my ribs. At the foot of the Pillar the situation became critical, for we couldn't risk crossing the col in a white out. We had no choice but to wait in the tents for a further two days before we could finally escape. I was very weak, coughing, and worried about catching pneumonia which would have finished me. Doug had to crawl across the col and descend the fixed ropes and then make a punishing three-mile crawl across glacier and moraine.

Doug Scott on the descent: jumaring up ropes to the West Summit (*inset*) and crawling down to the top of the Pillar.

After two days on the col the weather cleared and we completed our escape: Doug crawling across the col (*inset*) and abseiling down the fixed ropes.

Doug (on a makeshift stretcher) and I at Base Camp before the long journey back to Skardu.

7 K2 – End of an Era

The only trace of the avalanche was the cone of snow at the bottom of the hanging glacier, but that had been there before. It didn't seem any bigger, yet thousands of tons of snow and ice must have poured down, sweeping Nick with them. There were just a few puffy afternoon clouds in the sky, not a breath of wind. The triple summits of Broad Peak, the perfect snow pyramid of Angel Peak, and the great white sail of Skilbrum were tranquil under the hot afternoon sun.

Back in camp the survivors, Doug Scott, Peter Boardman, Joe Tasker, Jim Duff and I were grappling with grief, shock, guilt, relief at still being alive, trying to come to terms with what had happened. It was the end of an era. Nick had been one of my closest friends and a loyal support on Annapurna, Everest and now K2. Because of that very dependability I exploited his goodwill. I had counted on Nick, with Tut Braithwaite, to force the Rock Band on Everest in 1975, setting up Doug and Dougal for their summit bid. It was Nick who, after I had been left in Askole on the way back from the Ogre, stayed behind to organise my evacuation after everyone else had gone home. I still miss his friendship, the great gap-toothed grin, his capacity for enjoyment and the fun we had on British crags.

Nick's death marked the end of an era in a broader sense. As in any sport, there had been team changes because of personality or the cruel toll of death. In addition to Ian Clough and Mick Burke, Dougal Haston had died in an avalanche near his home in Switzerland. But the expedition formula itself was showing signs of stress. Doug Scott, a strong personality with his own ideas of running things, had gone along with the style of leadership I had used on Everest, but on K2 was obviously restive. On Everest in 1975 we had shown that a well structured expedition with sufficient resources can climb almost anything. The next logical challenge was to tackle increasingly difficult climbs with ever smaller expeditions. This was something that Doug was to do the following year with Pete Boardman, Joe Tasker and the French climber, Georges Bettembourg, when they made the first ascent of the North Ridge of Kangchenjunga.

I have never contemplated abandoning climbing, but immediately after the tragedy on K2 I lost my appetite for expeditioning, withdrew from a trip to Kang Taiga (Kangtega), which Nick and I had planned together, and plunged into researching and writing *Quest For Adventure*, a study of post-war adventure. It was the chance of climbing in China that re-kindled my enthusiasm.

In the mid-seventies, with access to the Karakoram easing after years of restrictions, the unclimbed ridges of K2 (28,253ft/8611m) were being considered by the various ambitious groups interested in the highest peaks. After our Everest adventures K2's immense West Ridge seemed the logical challenge. In some ways it was even more formidable than Everest's South-West Face, but we wanted to climb it with a smaller team than we had used in 1975 and so settled on just eight climbers and one high-altitude porter. From our Base Camp on the Savoia Glacier, the route followed a subsidiary glacier leading up to the West Face, and then up snow slopes towards the ridge. We placed Camp 1 below a rock buttress half-way up the slope and then crossed the upper snow slope, above the ice-fall, to the site of Camp 2, below the rock walls on the right flank of the ridge.

Distributing the daily flour ration and making chapattis.

K2, WEST RIDGE, 1978

The route to K2 up the Baltoro Glacier is one of the toughest expedition approaches in the whole of the Greater Himalaya, a week's walk from the nearest village, with five days over the tortuous humps of the rubble-strewn glacier. The arduousness of the journey is mitigated by the surroundings, as the approach passes below a number of difficult and spectacular peaks, including the Grand Cathedral, Masherbrum, the Trango Towers, Gasherbrum 4 and Broad Peak. Ten days' food for the entire porter force has to be carried beyond Askole and each night the ration of flour, rice, dahl and other items is shared out amongst the porters.

We established Base Camp on June 2 and by June 11 Pete Boardman and Joe Tasker were installed in Camp 2 and extending the route up the mixed ground on the flank of the ridge.

Porters congregate on the Baltoro at Urdukas below the Grand Cathedral.

A view down across the snow slope from Camp 2 taken just after the fateful avalanche.

At about midday, when I was resting at Camp 1 with Jim Duff, a huge avalanche poured over the ice cliffs to our right. With a reflex action I started to take photographs, until Jim shouted, "For God's sake stop! Nick and Doug could be in that." They had set out from the camp about two hours earlier to ferry loads to Camp 2. We tried to convince ourselves that the avalanche would have missed them, but about an hour later Doug rushed into the camp with news that Nick was dead.

Doug had been towing a long length of 5mm nylon rope across the snow slope to fix a handrail. He had reached the other side when the entire slope broke away in a windslab avalanche. Nick, who was in the middle of the slope, didn't have a chance of surviving. Doug, with the rope tied round his waist, was dragged back down towards the maelstrom, but was saved when the rope snapped leaving him at the very edge of the moving snow. Our expedition had ended in tragedy at its very beginning.

A long-focus view of the slopes between Camp 1 and Camp 2 with the avalanche scar clearly visible at the top of the snow slope.

The avalanche from Camp 1.

The last photograph of Nick Estcourt.

Mustagh Ata 24,758ft/7546m, towering above a
Kirghiz burial ground on the Sinkiang steppes,
was first climbed in 1956. The mountain is
considerably easier and lower than Kongur, yet
with its isolated charisma, it upstages its infinitely
more challenging neighbour.

8   Climbs from China

The hills were rounded, rising in stepped brown tiers, whilst the Karakol Lake was the deepest blue, reflecting the clarity of the sky. To the south was Mustagh Ata, a great cone of snow and glaciers rising out of the dusty brown foothills like an extinct volcano. Kongur was behind me, almost lost in the sweep of rounded snow peaks filling the eastern horizon. The fascination of climbing in China is not just in the unclimbed peaks, although there are plenty of them, it is more in a sense one has of wide horizons, cloud mountains that are often grander than the peaks themselves and the subtle colouring of even the bleakest scene. The rocks and baked ground are every shade of brown, red and grey and when you look closer you see they abound in life. Primulas and dwarf irises hide in the beds of dried out water courses or spring up in the wake of the departing snows.

The yurt (domed tent) of some Kirghiz, who were grazing their flocks of sheep and goats, nestled in a small valley. I was invited in by the head of the family who had the quiet courtesy of a nomad, but I wondered how much their lives had changed since the Revolution. In the past they had roamed between Russia and Sinkiang, ignoring national frontiers. But now they had gone through the process of collectivisation. In theory my hosts were members of a work brigade based on a characterless set of one-storey concrete buildings some miles away. With the relaxation that followed the death of Mao, they were allowed to own a proportion of their flocks. They also enjoyed the benefit of education and health care. But it was difficult to determine how content they were with their lot. They undoubtedly had much greater freedom than people in the cities. Even at the height of the Cultural Revolution the Chinese had shown greater restraint in their dealings with the various ethnic groups that made up the population of Sinkiang which is too close to the potentially hostile borders of the Soviet Union, with too many people of the same race on the other side of the frontier.

The Tibetans fared less well. When we visited Tibet for the first time in 1982 to attempt the North-East Ridge of Everest and again in 1987 and 1988 for Menlungtse, we were saddened by the havoc that had been wreaked on their culture, religion and national identity. Hundreds of monasteries had been destroyed and thousands of monks and other Tibetan leaders had been incarcerated in camps, many losing their lives. Their culture, too, had been attacked and for a time only Chinese was taught in their schools.

In 1982 Tibet had only just been opened to foreigners. The few monasteries

A view across the steppes to the Kongur massif, from the same position as the picture on the previous page, with Kongur Tiube (24,541ft/7480m) on the left and Kongur (25,325ft/7719m) peeping modestly above an intervening ridge to its right – its complexity totally disguised.

that had been spared were re-opened and treated as revenue-earners for the tourist industry. But Tibetans were now allowed into them as well, so in the Jokhang Temple there were great queues of Tibetans in the drab Chinese blue or green, as well as Kampas from distant parts with their plaited hair, turquoise necklaces, leather knee breeches, Tibetan boots and homespun jackets hanging off one shoulder; people, young and very old, prostrating over and over again in an atmosphere of fervent piety that showed Tibetan Buddhism was very much alive. A few monks had been allowed back into the surviving monasteries and there were even some young novices starting the path of learning.

In 1987 and 1988, in our attempts to climb Menlungtse, we were going to a region whose last foreign visitors had been members of the 1921 and 1924 Everest expeditions who crossed the Fushi La to explore the upper Rongshar Gorge on the southern side of the Himalayan watershed, close to the Nepalese frontier. The Tibetans of Rongshar have always had close links with the Sherpas and still slip back and forth across the frontier. The principal village, Changbujiang, was administered by the Communist village leader and a cadre of minor civil servants from a compound above and away from the village.

The village seemed to run its own affairs and even in the twelve months between our visits I observed a significant relaxation of control from the district headquarters, and an increase in private enterprise, particularly, and ominously, in the timber business. There is an insatiable demand for timber in Tibet, both for building and fuel. Although the hillside opposite the village was protected, there seemed little control of felling elsewhere and the superb pine forest in the Menlung valley was being decimated. The villagers were profiting in the short

term, cutting and transporting timber by yak. Between 1987 and 1988 the number of yaks they owned had tripled. Their living standards had also improved, with more wood-burning stoves in the houses and glass-paned windows, but in a few years' time the forest will be destroyed. These Tibetans were probably better off now than they had been before the Chinese invasion.

In both Sinkiang and Tibet we were always aware of the country's rigid centralist system. The very fact that we had with us a Han Chinese liaison officer and interpreter, that everything had to be organised through the Chinese Mountaineering Association and that we were largely insulated from direct contact with ordinary people, emphasised this fact. It was very different from climbing in Nepal, India or Pakistan where there are regulations and liaison officers, but expeditions are left to make their own arrangements, hire their own porters and purchase their own food.

In fairness, there were advantages in dealing with the CMA and over the years I have made some very good friends in the CMA and amongst Chinese mountaineers. They did their best to give us a smooth passage and stood by their regulations and price structure, though we sometimes had some long and convoluted arguments over their interpretation. It pays to read the small print while being careful to

Tibetan yak herders preparing tsampa feed cakes for their animals before a day's work. This supplement is given in the early spring to fortify yaks weakened by the lack of forage through the winter.

A statue of Mao Tse-tung dominated Kashgar but he had to share the portrait gallery below with the newly appointed Chairman Hua, soon to be deposed by Premier Deng.

remain cool and avoid confrontational stances. It is important for Chinese not to lose face and that there is always the possibility of a compromise acceptable to both parties. It makes life much easier if you accept the fact that the Chinese regard expeditioning as a means of earning much needed foreign currency and make sure you take enough money.

Because of this, most expeditions climbing in China need some form of sponsorship. It is always easier to find sponsorship for a superlative – for the first or the highest. We had little trouble in finding a sponsor, Jardine Matheson, for Kongur, for it was the first major British expedition to get into China since the war and it was going for one of the highest unclimbed peaks in the world. The company, which has historic Chinese trading links, was so pleased with the results of its sponsorship that it supported us on our subsequent venture to the North-East Ridge of Everest.

Menlungtse, however, offered some problems. It was certainly one of the most attractive unclimbed peaks in the world, but at 23,560ft (7181m) it was comparatively modest in stature. We were lucky in 1987 to be supported by the Norwegian Export Finance Council, mainly through the personal contact of one of the Norwegian team members (personal contact is one of the most important factors in gaining sponsorship). But in 1988 our chances of getting sponsorship for the mountain seemed thin. It was the Yeti that came to our rescue.

In 1951 Eric Shipton and Michael Ward, at the end of the Everest Reconnaissance expedition, crossed a pass leading into Tibet at the head of the Menlung valley, walking down it to the Rongshar Gorge and on to the Nepalese frontier. At the head of the Menlung Glacier they photographed some tracks which became the best evidence of the Yeti's existence. At the end of our 1987 expedition we saw and photographed some tracks further down the Menlung valley. They certainly looked like those of a two-legged creature, though whether these were of the Yeti is far from conclusive. But there was a great deal of interest in them when we got back home and, as a result, we were able to cover our costs entirely. I came in for a fair amount of good-natured leg-pulling in the climbing press and the national media, but our sponsors got a good story and we were able to tackle our mountain.

Kirghiz families at their summer grazing camp at Tugnakunush on the east side of Kongur, with their yurt behind them and mountains of the Tigarman Range in the background.

Uighur school children on parade in Urumchi, capital of Sinkiang.

Kirghiz horsemen playing Buzkashi with a goat skin, a very rough and egalitarian forerunner of polo that was originally played with a live goat.

Mike Ward and Shi Zhanchun, Chairman of the CMA, sign the protocol in Beijing.

China had been closed to western climbers since the Communist takeover but after Mao's death it was clear that restrictions might ease. After diplomatic moves in London during Chairman Hua's visit, Mike Ward and I were sent out by the Mount Everest Foundation to negotiate with the CMA. At the same time eight mountains were offered for visiting expeditions but the only major unclimbed peak was Kongur which was also one of the highest unclimbed peaks in the world. We therefore secured an early permission for that objective. Costs were high, necessitating powerful

Kongur hiding behind Junction Peak (7350m) which w reconnaissance, we seriously underestimated the complex

(*above*) The reconnaissance party with a CMA welcoming delegation at Urumchi airport, and working out the sponsorship terms with Jardine Matheson officials in Hong Kong (*below*) – David Newbigging, the Taipan of the company, is on the right.

sponsorship. This was provided by Jardine Matheson, a large company with heavy Chinese interests. Because so little was known about the mountain Mike Ward, Al Rouse and I conducted a reconnaissance in 1980, making two minor first ascents in the process. The main expedition in 1981 had both a scientific and a climbing objective. The team numbered ten but only four of us (Rouse and myself, plus Pete Boardman and Joe Tasker) were to attempt the mountain — in alpine-style.

(*right*) All in the name of science — physiological torture administered by Doctors Jim Milledge and Mike Ward to Pete Boardman.

...ss to tackle the summit pyramid. Despite our thorough ...mb.

KONGUR (continued)

The approach climb up the South Ridge of Junction Peak proved harder than expected and we had three bivouacs before crossing the top. After establishing a good snow cave on the col beyond, we attempted the summit pyramid making some progress. But with the weather unsettled and food running out, we were compelled to retreat down the easier West Ridge.

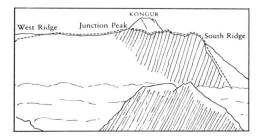

Our camp at the foot of the South Ridge of Junction Peak with an unclimbed 6000-metre peak in the background.

Joe Tasker approaching the summit of Junction Peak after our arduous ascent of the South Ridge. Mustagh Ata is in the background on the right.

By the entrance of the snow cave on the col.

Inside our four-man snow cave – five-star comfort in a deep freeze!

KONGUR (continued)

Snow caves were a vital factor in our success. They gave more effective shelter from the wind than tents and enabled us to reduce the weight of our equipment. Our main four-man hole on the col enabled us to plan and reach decisions together. This provided a launch point for our second summit bid. We had hoped to find a site for another cave at the end of the knife-edged ridge that led from the col to the summit pyramid, but there was insufficient snow and we were only able to scoop out a series of slots or 'coffins' just large enough for one person to lie in. We were trapped here by a four-day storm, but resolved to wait and go for the summit, even though we were nearly out of food.

(*below*) On the linking ridge, approaching the gendarme. (*above right*) Joe Tasker in his 'snow coffin'. The ceiling was just a few inches thick.

Two views of the sustained mixed climbing on the final pyramid, on ground reminiscent of the North Face of the Matterhorn.

KONGUR (continued)

We were trapped in the coffins for four days by a violent storm. It was a serious situation, yet there was never any thought of retreat. On the fifth morning the weather cleared and we set out for the summit. It was bitterly cold, we were weakened by our four days of inactivity on half rations and the climbing on the northern flank was

The summit pyramid of Kongur. The snow cave was on the col in the foreground and the coffin camp was beyond the gendarme on the linking ridge.

The summit at last – or so we thought! Pete and Al on the last few feet.

intimidating. Fortunately, after four pitches, we were able to gain the crest of the ridge where easier ground led on to the summit, which we reached just before dusk, where we dug a snow cave. On the following morning, another top, about a mile away, seemed higher than the one we were on. We therefore trekked across to it, only to find that it was lower.

We then began the descent.

During one of the abseils Pete Boardman was hit on the head by a football-sized rock and slid out of sight, unconscious. Luckily he came to rest in soft snow but for a moment it looked as if we might have another Ogre-like crisis on our hands. However he recovered sufficiently to reach the snow cave on the col, and after a night's rest was fit enough for the final descent.

KONGUR (continued)

It had been a committing but very satisfying climb on a mountain that turned out to be both complex and difficult. We spent eight nights above 24,000ft and were very fortunate not to be hit by another storm. If Pete had been seriously injured we would have had a desperate time getting him over Junction Peak and back to safety. We had drawn on all our reserves of strength, experience and luck, climbed the mountain and returned safely.

(*above*) Tired after our sustained climb, and with the weather deteriorating we slogged back over Junction Peak.

(*left*) Joe Tasker, myself, Pete Boardman and Al Rouse on the Koksel Glacier after a safe return from our ten-day trip.

On Everest we wanted to use the same tactics that we had employed so successfully on Kongur. The team was almost the same (Dick Renshaw taking Al Rouse's place), with just two support climbers, Dr Charles Clarke and Adrian Gordon.

There is a sense of history about the northern side of the mountain. This was the scene of the many pre-war attempts from the North Col and of Mallory and Irvine's celebrated last climb when, after they were last seen moving up into the clouds at 28,000ft/8500m, they might just have reached the top. The mountain was eventually climbed from this side in 1960 by the Chinese who initially tried the North-East Ridge but eventually

Pete Boardman and Dick Renshaw planning our route at Advance Base.

used the North Col route.

This joins the North-East Ridge at the 8000-metre level and, in 1982, the complete ridge was one of the most obvious remaining challenges on the

mountain. We felt that it could be climbed by a small team without using oxygen. It was exposed to the wind, had great length, there was a series of difficult pinnacles barring the way to the traditional route, and then there was the upper section that had confounded all the pre-war teams — a combination of difficulties that made it a very serious challenge, the key factor being the debilitating length of time that a small team would need to spend at high altitude. Nevertheless after Kongur we were very confident and whilst I had private doubts about my own ability to press on to the top without oxygen, I wanted to be part of such a challenging enterprise, and was fully prepared to drop back in support if I weakened.

Everest from the north, showing the line of the then unclimbed North-East Ridge up the left-hand skyline. The Pinnacles are half-way along the ridge and the North Col route joins the ridge just above them.

The Potala, former palace of the Dalai Lama, rising above the drab office and apartment buildings of the new Lhasa.

EVEREST, NORTH-EAST RIDGE (continued)

Tibet had been open to foreigners for two years when we arrived in Lhasa. Although many dreary modern buildings had been erected and the city was surrounded by army camps, it still had special magic of its own. Over 2000 monasteries had been destroyed during the Cultural Revolution, many of the monks had been imprisoned and all forms of religious expression had been prohibited. A few of the major monasteries had been spared and some monks had been allowed back but it was a tiny proportion of those that had been there before. Originally there had been 11,000 monks in the Drepung Monastery and now there were only a few hundred. The Chinese seem to regard these places as useful tourist attractions and money earners, but the Tibetans still hold them in awe as places of worship, queuing to visit them in their hundreds. There was an extraordinary feeling of devoutness, that Tibetan Buddhism was still very much alive.

Pilgrims, some of whom have travelled from the furthest reaches of Tibet, patiently queuing in the Jokhang Temple.

There is a fascinating blend of modern and traditional styles in Lhasa.

Resting on the steps of the Potala after a long pilgrimage.

EVEREST, NORTH-EAST RIDGE (continued)

We moved on to Xigaze, Tibet's second city. Here the monks of the Tashilumpo Monastery were busy preparing for a religious festival. We then went to Xegur from where trucks took us to the Everest Base Camp. This slow approach to the mountain was essential to help us to acclimatise.

Monks in the courtyard of the Tashilumpo Monastery preparing sacred tsampa cakes to distribute to the pilgrims.

Nearing the site of Advance Base. The North-East Ridge is the skyline on the left and the North Col is on the right.

EVEREST, NORTH-EAST
RIDGE (continued)

We established Advance Base
(20,342ft/6200m) on the
East Rongbuk Glacier on
April 4. In biting cold with a
penetrating wind, we pushed
the route forward, establishing
three snow hole camps, the
highest at 25,755ft/7850m
just below the Pinnacles that
were clearly going to be the
crux of the route. The
climbing to that point was
not difficult but length of the
ridge, the altitude, the
remorseless wind and the
lack of fixed rope, all
combined to make it a
gruelling experience.

On the lower part of the ridge with Chomo Lonzo in the background.

Approaching the rock steps, turned on the right, between snow hole Camps 2 and 3.

A view across the immense snow sweeps of the Kangshung Face from the site of Camp 3 (our third snow hole).

The steepening ridge leading to the Pinnacles above Camp 3 with the North Col below on the right. Our attempts on this were interrupted by Dick Renshaw's stroke and we had to make a hasty unplanned retreat (*inset*) to Advance Base.

EVEREST, NORTH-EAST RIDGE (continued)

The plan was to get the route established to the top of the First Pinnacle as a jumping-off point for an alpine-style dash for the summit. Whilst fixing rope up to this point, Dick Renshaw suffered a mild stroke, brought on by the effects of altitude, and we were forced to withdraw to Base at a critical stage. Dick left for home, and I too realised I didn't have the strength to return for the final climb. Thus the depleted team of Pete Boardman and Joe Tasker set out on May 15 to attempt to cross the Pinnacles. They made their last radio call on the evening of May 16. We watched their progress over the Pinnacles throughout the following day and at 9pm saw them for the last time, passing out of sight behind the Second Pinnacle. The following day Adrian Gordon and I climbed up to the North Col in a prearranged plan to support Pete and Joe on their descent.

(*left*) Boardman, Tasker and Renshaw pushing the route out towards the First Pinnacle.

(*below*) Pete Boardman and Joe Tasker leaving Advance Base on the final climb.

From Advance Base Camp we could just see them as two tiny dots approaching the Second Pinnacle on the evening of May 17.

Joe Tasker and Pete Boardman.

Adrian Gordon leading up to the North Col.

EVEREST, NORTH-EAST RIDGE
(continued)

We waited on the North Col, and with no more sightings of the climbers, it was clear that something had gone wrong. After four days we descended and later studied the Kangshung Face for clues but saw nothing. What happened remains a mystery: they may have slipped and fallen or succumbed to exhaustion during a bivouac.

Adrian studying the mountain from the North Col after three days of waiting.

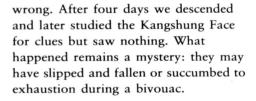

Menlungtse from the south, the West Peak is on the left and the main East Peak on the right.
Our 1985 route took the spur of West Peak on the extreme left.

MENLUNGTSE, 1987–88

Menlungtse, standing just inside Tibet, though south of the Himalayan watershed, has tantalised mountaineers ever since the late forties. At that time the first expeditions were allowed into Nepal and climbers operating in the Everest region saw to the west this magnificent obelisk of grey granite coated in snow. Following their Everest reconnaissance in 1951 Eric Shipton and Mike Ward returned by a cross-country route that took in the head of the Menlung valley where they studied the peak and also photographed some

tracks which have become the best evidence available of the existence of the Yeti.

I first saw Menlungtse from Nuptse in 1961 and was again reminded of it during our Everest trips in the seventies and slowly a desire grew to climb it. Having established a good relationship with the CMA, I successfully applied for permission to attempt the peak in 1987 with an Anglo–Norwegian team comprising Jim Fotheringham, Odd Eliassen and Bjorn Myrer-Lund, with a small support group.

We entered Tibet from Nepal by the main road linking Kathmandu with

Lhasa. Previously all access to Tibet had been through Beijing but by the mid-eighties the regulations had eased to allow this more convenient approach. We travelled by truck over the high Tibetan plateau, past the village of Tingri, to the roadhead (4800m) just north of the Nangpa La from where we continued using yaks. There is one major disadvantage with this approach. The very fast height gain, first over a 6000-metre pass and then across the high Tibetan plateau to the roadhead presented serious acclimatisation problems and three members of the team suffered from altitude sickness.

Villagers of Tingri celebrating the Tibetan New Year.

The 'bracing' lorry trip across the Tibetan plateau.

A solar power device for boiling kettles in Tingri.

Our yak column heading south to the northern end of the Nangpa La where we turned westwards to the Fushi La to enter the Rongshar valley.

Crossing the Fushi La with Cho Oyu and the Nangpa La in the background.

Children of Changbujiang in the Rongshar valley.

MENLUNGTSE (continued)

To reach Menlungtse we had to recross the watershed by the Fushi La (5400m) to gain the Rongshar valley. On this trip we saw much more of the ordinary people of Tibet. The peasants owned their own yaks and crops.

Changbujiang had a boom economy because of the demand for timber, but this will soon present serious problems of deforestation unless wood-cutting is more closely controlled. We established Base Camp in late March and reconnoitred the mountain, selecting the buttress sweeping up from the right-hand corner of the picture below. It presented technically hard rock climbing with few bivouac sites. On our first attempt we ran out about a thousand feet of fixed rope and then made an alpine-style push with three bivouacs reaching the start of the snow ridge about half-way up the picture at around 6400m.

Jim Fotheringham.

Menlungtse West from the south-west showing the routes of 1987 and 1988.

Odd Eliassen.

Bjorn Myrer-Lund.

On the Buttress between Camps 1 and 2. The initial looseness gave way to fine climbing on solid granite.

Bjorn Myrer-Lund on the difficult slabs (5a/5.9) half-way up the Buttress.

Jim Fotheringham scans prices in the *Financial Times* at our campsite.

We reached our high point, at the top of the steep section of the Buttress, in the second week of April. Clouds were building up over Nepal and there was the distant crash of thunder. While Jim and Bjorn pushed the route out fixing all our ropes for a quick start the following day, Odd and I prepared the camp to withstand the tempest. It hit us before we were ready and we finished putting up the tents in a vicious thunderstorm. Jim was hit by a lightning bolt and collapsed unconscious for a few seconds. We piled into the hurriedly pitched tents, tried to clear them of the snow that had poured in and spent a precarious night battered by ferocious winds. By morning the Norwegians' tent had been ripped to bits and we had no choice but to retreat.

I jumared up to retrieve the ropes fixed the previous night and started to follow the others who had already completed the first abseil. Leaning off a snow stake to reach the first anchor, I was horrified when the stake pulled straight out, catapulting me down the slope. It was only with a violent heave that I reached out and grabbed the secured abseil rope, just managing to hang on.

We returned twice to the ridge, each time reaching the high point and each time were forced back by violent storms. 1987 was a bad season throughout Nepal.

We turned the final section of the Buttress by climbing the ice face on its left flank which led to the crest of the snow ridge above.

Jim making himself comfortable on our second bivouac ledge.

An abseil retreat down dangerous broken ground in a storm.

On the lower part of the West Face.

MENLUNGTSE (continued)

I returned in 1988 with an Anglo–American team of David Breashears, Steve Shea, Andy Fanshawe, Alan Hinkes, with Charlie Clarke and Jess Stock in support. We attempted the West Ridge alpine-style, but turned back, largely because of lack of acclimatisation, at about 6700m, just below the final headwall. I was slow to recover from this attempt – age at last beginning to take its toll? – and therefore stood down, whilst Hinkes and Fanshawe made a second bold and successful attempt, reaching the West Summit.

(*left*) Steve Shea sets out on the first of a series of sustained pitches on the upper ice-field on the West Face with Andy Fanshawe and Dave Breashears in support. The ice-field, as big as any of the famous alpine faces, led to the rock headwall where we hoped to climb an ice runnel or gully. This attempt failed but the face was subsequently climbed by Fanshawe and Alan Hinkes (*inset*).

9 Snatched Opportunities

A typical example of an unexpected opportunity came in 1971 when, after various other projects had fallen through, I received an invitation from the American climbers Tom Frost, Jim McCarthy and Sandy Bill to join them on an attempt on the unclimbed East Face of the Moose's Tooth (10,335ft/ 3150m) in Alaska (*left*).

Jim McCarthy had just got his pilot's licence so we flew to Alaska from New York in his Cessna aircraft with me in the role of navigator. The flight took a week and the entire trip was worth it for this experience alone. We didn't get far up the Moose's Tooth, being rained off after a thousand feet of technical rock climbing on the steep rock apron at the base of this huge face. It was here that I was introduced to the systematic big-wall techniques developed by American climbers in Yosemite valley. The face was eventually climbed by Jim Bridwell and Mugs Stump who outflanked the lower apron by a line further to the right. They solved the problems of rain and wet snow that plague the lower peaks of Alaska by doing the climb in winter.

You need to be something of an opportunist to be a successful climber. On the hill you need to seize every possible chance, from a turn in the weather to a change of line on the route. There's the satisfaction of grabbing a climb between spells of bad weather and making it back to the hut or camp just before the storm rolls in or, nearer home, getting out for an evening climb and finishing in time for a pint before the pub closes. It's an aspect of the innate competitive instinct that is within the psyche of so many climbers, but it's a competition with time and fortune as much as one's fellows.

The way I earn a living is essentially sedentary, by writing, lecturing or broadcasting, though as most of my material is provided by climbing, this gives me a good excuse to get out as often as possible. Some of the most enjoyable experiences I've had have been when I have squeezed a quick climb into a tight schedule, when a lecture tour or conference has taken me to a mountainous part of the world or a surprise invitation suddenly arrives. It has made new friendships for me all over the world, that can be picked up again over a long period of time. There is a spontaneity about such an enterprise missing from the painstaking preparation needed for a major expedition and there's a sense of fun from the very beginning, even if the climb itself turns into an epic.

Success on these ventures is always the aim but failure need not be an anti-climax. Take the Moose's Tooth in Alaska; in climbing terms we achieved comparatively little, but as an experience it was a delight, cementing friendships that have lasted to this day. Mount Cook was a classic route, but the very elegance of our fast ascent in a part of New Zealand where people can often wait weeks to do a climb because of the bad weather, gave it an added value.

Our ascent of Shivling, which I tacked onto a mountaineering conference in Delhi, was one of the best climbing trips I have had. The boldness of the climb, the smallness of the team, and the way we snatched success out of what could easily have been a complete non-event all added up to a superb adventure.

I shall always be grateful to Frank Wells and Dick Bass for inviting me to Mount Vinson, but also a little guilty for bagging the summit by myself when the others retreated, even though standing on the highest point of Antarctica was one of the strongest experiences in my life, my own solitude enhancing the empty loneliness and beauty of those stark sterile mountains and the vastness of the ice-cap.

On the Moose's Tooth: Tom Frost climbing (*left*) and Jim McCarthy and I, soaked to the skin after our first bivouac (*below*).

Dawn on the East Ridge of Mount Cook, one of the great classic climbs of New Zealand.

On a tight schedule, we flew to the plateau below Mount Cook.

MOUNT COOK, EAST RIDGE, 1976

After a lecture booking in Christchurch, New Zealand, I was able to fill the three days before my return flight to Britain with a quick visit to the Mount Cook region. With Nick Banks and two of his friends, all Everesters, we flew in to a high plateau and the following morning completed the classic East Ridge of Mount Cook (12,349ft/3764m). We also climbed the Symes Ridge of Mount Tasman.

The mountains of New Zealand provide a more challenging training ground than the Alps. The weather is unpredictable, the mountains heavily glaciated and there are fewer huts. With such a fine local area it is hardly surprising that New Zealand mountaineers have made such an impact on world climbing.

The North Face of Shivling (21,467ft/6,543m) in the Gangotri region. The North-East Ridge on the left was first climbed by a party led by Doug Scott in 1981. We used the middle section of unclimbed North Ridge on the right-hand skyline as our descent route.

SHIVLING, 1983

Invitations to a mountaineering conference in India gave Jim Fotheringham and me free air flights and a chance to snatch a Himalayan climb. We choose the Gangotri region with its fine steep mountains of around 21,000ft/6500m. The town of Gangotri is reached by bus, and a three-day walk led on to the mountains. We had hoped to tackle the huge granite wall of the East Face of Kedarnath Dome, a sort of Gangotri El Capitan, but on close inspection we decided it was too big for the time available and for a two-man team. We therefore opted for our

second objective, the unclimbed South-West Summit of Shivling, by its South-East Ridge. This presented an alpine-style challenge in the fullest sense. We made a recce one afternoon but were only able to see the lower ramparts of the mountain because of cloud. To add to the uncertainty we had only the vaguest knowledge of the first ascent route on the other side of the East Summit, which we would probably have to use for descent.

We took food for five days, a small tent, an MSR kerosene stove and a rack of rock and ice equipment. Our sacks weighed about fifteen kilos. The start was formidable, with a rampart of

crumbling rock walls, ice cliffs and evil-looking gullies barring the way. The only feasible route took a wide snow gully leading up below a threatening overhanging ice wall. A rock the size of a Volkswagen came rattling down when we were in the gully and, with nowhere to shelter, we just froze as it rumbled past, bouncing against the gully walls. Somewhat chastened, we rushed, lungs straining, up the rest of the gully to where a fork led out of the danger area, but thereby became fully committed with no desire to go back down the same route.

Shivling from the south with the South-West Summit on the left and our ridge to the immediate right of the shaded face. Access to the ridge was by a sinister couloir (*below*) threatened by a large ice cliff.

We made haste up the couloir (*inset*) until level with the ice cliff.

Jim Fotheringham considering our prospects from the first bivouac ledge.

On the main rock ridge the climbing was around Severe (4b/5.5) on superb grey granite. It was impossible to sack-haul, so on the harder pitches the leader climbed without a sack and abseiled back down to retrieve it. The climb began to feel very committing for retreat would have been difficult and dangerous. On our fourth day we only made about 400ft before pitching our tent. The crux, an overhanging corner (5b/5.9), was just beyond, and after this broken ground led on to the summit ridge where we bivouacked, going on to the top on the morning of the sixth day.

Climbing up to the crest of the ridge. The pedestal of our third bivouac (*inset below*) can be seen on the crest.

On the ridge the second man often jumared carrying the heavier pack.

Jim leading the crux corner – not easy in double-boots!

Our fourth bivouac, just below the crux, with Meru in the background.

(*above*) Looking down from below the summit tower as Jim descends past the bivouac site and down towards the col, all on avalanche-prone slopes. From the col we followed the line of the bergschrund across to the left to continue our complex descent on unknown ground.

(*left*) From our fifth bivouac we moved up the crest of the mountain to the sharpest Himalayan top I've ever climbed.

We built a secure Base Camp on the Antarctic Plateau at a height of about 8000 feet. The modified three-engined DC3 is securely tethered to prevent it blowing away in a storm.

MOUNT VINSON, 1983

A chance meeting with two wealthy Americans below Everest in 1982 led to my ascent of Mount Vinson (16,860ft/5140m), the highest mountain in Antarctica. Frank Wells and Dick Bass were trying to climb the highest point of all seven continents in the space of a single year, and they invited me to join them on Mount Vinson. The climbing was not difficult but the isolation of the mountain, combined with the bitter cold and wind, made it feel serious. We had twenty-four hours of daylight, but it required three camps to get within striking distance of the summit. On the first attempt I pushed on to the summit when the others faltered in the face of savage winds, but they completed the climb a few days later.

On the summit bid the others were forced ba[ck]

Sledge-hauling towards the Vinson Massif.

Rick Ridgeway, my climbing partner.

Seven-summitteers – Frank Wells (*left*) and Dick Bass (*right*).

...nd and cold, leaving Ridgeway and myself to go on (*above*). Then he dropped back and I continued alone to the top (*inset*) of the loneliest continent on earth.

A few days later the others reached the top (*right*) using face masks as protection against the biting winds.

IO   Everest – a Fulfilment

Arne Naess, leader of the
Norwegian Everest expedition.

I used a battery and solar-powered
computer to write my newspaper
despatches from the mountain.

Almost every climber, I suspect, dreams in his heart of hearts of standing on the summit of Everest. For some it might be no more than an idle fantasy, for others a driving force. The strength of the attraction is easy to understand – reaching the heights fits in with so many metaphors, but the summit experience on any peak is ephemeral, the excitement of that unique panoramic view all too often clouded by worries about how you're going to get back down. The satisfaction of a climb completed comes later. There is an intellectual challenge of a problem solved, exploration, finding a new way up a mountain that has perhaps never been climbed. Gratification of ego, the effort you have put in, the risks taken, and perhaps as important as any of these, how well you get on with your fellow climbers, how much you gave as well as took, that sense of sharing that makes an experience all the richer.

There was nothing new in my ascent of Everest. Ours was the sixty-sixth ascent. We were using oxygen, had a strong Sherpa team and climbed the mountain by its most popular route, the South-East Ridge, sometimes dismissively referred to as the 'yak route'. Yet it is a fine classic route that builds up to a crescendo from the departure from the South Col by the light of head torches in the dark, the plod over rocky steps and up snow gullies to reach the South-East Shoulder with the dawn, the long sweep of the arête up to the South Summit, and then the shock of seeing the knife-edged, heavily corniced ridge reaching across to the steep snow of the Hillary Step – not surprising that Evans and Bourdillon balked when they made the first summit bid in 1953. Then the summit itself, with its incredible view of the Tibetan Plateau stretching in an ocean of rolling brown hills with the occasional white cap filling the northern segment of the firmament, Kangchenjunga far to the east, Nuptse, the mountain I had climbed twenty-four years before, now far below me on the other side of the Western Cwm. This really felt the highest place on earth.

The experience was enhanced by being part of a united and happy team and climbing with Pertemba who contributed so much to our success in 1975. I was exhausted and deeply moved by emotion, my mind filled with thoughts of so many friends who had died on Everest and elsewhere. The satisfaction came afterward, and it is still strong four years later, that feeling of having stood on the highest point of

Approaching the Hillary Step with the view down to the right to Tibet.

earth, that you can go no higher, no further, and the whole world is stretched out beneath. In a curious way it ended one chapter in my life and opened another. I was now free to look further afield, to the smaller but no less challenging unclimbed peaks that can still be found in the Greater Himalayan range and on the high Tibetan Plateau. There is still much to be done. Mountaineering in all its forms sustains a deep and satisfying challenge which, for me, is as fresh today as when I started, over thirty years ago.

EVEREST, SOUTH-EAST RIDGE, 1985

I was invited to join the Norwegian Everest expedition led by Arne Naess, and though initially I declined, shattered by the tragedy in 1982, eventually the lure was too great and I accepted. The initial summit bid failed and I made my attempt as part of a second group comprising Odd Eliassen, Bjorn Myrer-Lund, Dawa Nuru, Ang Lhakpa and Pertemba, again our sirdar, as in 1975. Our ascent by the traditional route was slow but orderly and made in perfect weather which was just as well as, even with oxygen, I found it exhausting. Pertemba brought the club shirt that Pete Boardman had worn in 1975 – it was a poignant reminder of lost friends that heightened the impact of an emotional ascent. A week later most of the other members of the expedition reached the summit as well.

Pictures of the summit climb (*clockwise from below*): Approaching the South Summit; Eliassen and Myrer-Lund moving off after an oxygen change; Pertemba and I on the steep slope below the South Summit; I move slowly up the final slope to the summit; (*inset*) Celebrating a successful ascent.

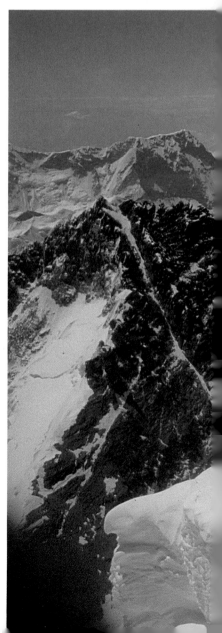

Climbing Record

Symbols: * *first ascent*, *w *first winter ascent*, † *first British ascent*.

1951 Ash Tree Gully *Dinas Bach* (Tom Blackburn) – first climb; Hope *Idwal Slabs* (Charles Verender) – first lead.

1952 Chimney Route *Clogwyn Du'r Arddu* (Dave Pullin); Rana Temporia *Quinag** (Tony) – first new route, a VS.

1953 Agag's Groove *Buachaille Etive Mor **w (Hamish MacInnes, Kerr McPhaill, John Hammond, G. McIntosh) – first winter climb; Crowberry Ridge Direct *w and Raven's Gully *Buachaille Etive Mor **w (Hamish MacInnes); Hangover *Clogwyn y Grochan* (Geoff Francis) – first 'Brown' route.

1954 Surplomb *Clogwyn y Grochan* (Steve Lane) – second ascent.

1955 Mercavity *Avon Gorge** (Geoff Francis) – first new route on Avon's Main Wall.

1957 First alpine season: South-East Face of Aig. du Tacul* (Hamish MacInnes), Steger Route *Cattinacio* and Yellow Edge and Demuth Route *Tre Cime* (Jim Swallow); North Wall Direct of Cima Una† (German climber). Malbogies *Avon Gorge** (Geoff Francis, Henry Rogers).

1958 Bonatti Pillar of Petit Dru† (Hamish MacInnes, Don Whillans and Paul Ross, with Walter Phillip and Richard Blach); West Face of Petites Jorasses† (Ronnie Wathen).

1959 Comici/Dimai, Brandler/Hasse† and Cassin/Ratti routes *Tre Cime* (Gunn Clark); Woubits (Jim O'Neill) and Mostest (Jim Swallow) *Clogwyn Du'r Arddu* – second ascents.

1960 Annapurna 2* by West Ridge *Nepal* (Dick Grant and Ang Nyima) – expedition led by Col. James Roberts; King Cobra *Skye** (Tom Patey).

1961 Nuptse* by South Face *Nepal* (part of second summit team with Jim Swallow, Ang Pemba and Les Brown – first pair: Dennis Davis and Tashi) – expedition led by Joe Walmsley; Central Pillar of Frêney, Mt. Blanc* (Don Whillans, Ian Clough and Jan Djuglosz).

1962 Trango *Castell Cidwm** (Joe Brown); Ichabod *Scafell* (Mike Thompson) – second ascent; Schmid/Krebs Route *Karwendal†* (Don Whillans); Walker Spur of Grandes Jorasses (Ian Clough); North Wall of the Eiger† (Ian Clough)

1963 Central Tower of Paine* by West Face *Chile* (Don Whillans) – expedition led by Barrie Page.

1964 North Face of Pointe Migot* and West Ridge of Aig. de Lepiney* (Tom Patey, Joe Brown and Robin Ford); Andrich/Fae Route on Civetta (Jim McCarthy); Medlar* (Martin Boysen) and Totalitarian* (Mike Thompson) *Raven Crag, Thirlmere*.

1965 Coronation Street *Cheddar** (Tony Greenbank); The Holy Ghost *Scafell** (Mike Thompson); West Face of the Cardinal* (Tom Patey and another); West Face Direct of Aig. du Plan* (Lito Tejada Flores); North-East Ridge of Dent du Midi* (Rusty Baillie and John Harlin); Right-Hand Pillar of Brouillard, Mt. Blanc* (Rusty Baillie, John Harlin and Brian Robertson).

1966 North Face Direct of the Eiger* – in supporting role; Old Man of Hoy *Orkneys** (Tom Patey and Rusty Baillie).

1968 North Face of Aig. d'Argentiere (Dougal Haston) – in winter.

1969 March Hare's Gully *Applecross **w (Tom Patey); Great Gully of Garbh Bheinn *w (Tom Patey and Don Whillans)

1970 South Face of Annapurna *Nepal** – leader of expedition – summit reached by Dougal Haston and Don Whillans.

1971 East Face of Moose's Tooth *Alaska* – attempt with Jim McCarthy Tom Frost and Sandy Bill curtailed by bad weather; White Wizard *Scafell** (Nick Estcourt)

1972 South-West Face of Everest *Nepal* – leader of expedition curtailed by cold and high wind; Great Gully of Grandes Jorasses (Dougal Haston with Mick Burke and Bev Clarke in support) – attempt in winter.

1973 Brammah* by the South Ridge *India* (Nick Escourt) – joint leader of expedition with Balwant Sandhu.

1974 Changabang* by East Ridge *India* (Martin Boysen, Doug Scott, Dougal Haston, Tashi and Balwant Sandhu) – joint leader of expedition with Sandhu.

1975 North Face Direct of Aig. du Triolet *w (Dougal Haston); South-West Face of Everest *Nepal** – leader of expedition – summit reached by Dougal Haston and Doug Scott, Pete Boardman, Pertemba and Mick Burke(?).

1976 North Face of Pt.20,309 *Kistwar, India* (Ronnie Richards) – attempt gaining two-thirds height; East Ridge of Mt. Cook and Symes Ridge of Mt. Tasman *New Zealand* (Nick Banks, Keith Woodford and Bob Cunningham).

1977 The Ogre* by the South Face *Pakistan* (Nick Escourt) and the West Ridge (Doug Scott) – the South Face climb ended at the West Summit. Clive Rowland and Mo Anthoine took part in the West Ridge ascent to the foot of the summit tower.

1978 West Ridge of K2 *Pakistan* – leader of expedition curtailed after death of Nick Escourt in an avalanche below Camp 2.

1980 Pts 6200m* and 5400* *Kongur Group, China* (Al Rouse and Mike Ward) – climbed during a reconnaissance expedition.

1981 Kongur* by the West Ridge *China* (Al Rouse, Pete Boardman and Joe Tasker) – expedition led by Mike Ward.

1982 North-East Ridge of Everest *Tibet* – leader of expedition curtailed after disappearance of Pete Boardman and Joe Tasker.

1983 Orion Face of Ben Nevis (Stuart Fife); South-West Summit of Shivling* by the South-East Ridge *India* (Jim Fotheringham); Mt. Vinson *Antarctica†* (Dick Bass, Tae Maeda, Yuichiro Miura, Steve Marts, Rick Ridgeway and Frank Wells) – soloed final section prior to ascent by the others. Expedition led jointly by Bass and Wells.

1984 West Ridge of Karun Koh *Pakistan* (Ikram Khan, Maqsood Ahmed and Al Rouse) – leader of expedition curtailed by bad weather; Cruel Sister *Pavey Ark* (Jim Loxham) – first E3 lead.

1985 South-East Ridge of Everest *Nepal* (Odd Eliassen, Bjorn Myrer Lund, Pertemba, Ang Lhakpa and Dawa Neru) – expedition led by Arne Naess.

1986 North-East Pillar of Norliga Skagastozstind *Norway* (Odd Eliassen); Athanor *Goat Crag* (Dave Absalom) – first 6a lead. Yellow Edge *Avon Gorge* (Steve Berry); South Pillar of Grosse Drusenturm *Rätikon* and North-East Diedre of Brenta Alta (Jim Fotheringham).

1987 South-West Buttress of Menlungtse West *Tibet* – leader of expedition curtailed by bad weather.

1987 Menlungtse West* by the West Ridge and Face *Tibet* – leader of expedition – summit reached by Andy Fanshawe and Alan Hinkes.

Books Detailed accounts of most of the climbs made before 1987 are in one or more of the following books: *I Chose to Climb* (Gollancz, 1966); *Annapurna South Face* (Cassell, 1971); *Everest, South-West Face* (Hodder and Stoughton, 1973); *The Next Horizon* (Gollancz, 1973); *Changabang* (Heinemann, 1975); *Everest the Hard Way* (Hodder and Stoughton, 1976); *Kongur* (Hodder and Stoughton, 1982); *Everest, The Unclimbed Ridge* (Hodder and Stoughton, 1983); *The Everest Years* (Hodder and Stoughton, 1986).

Photography I changed to Olympus cameras in 1974 with the introduction of its compact single lens reflex system. All my pictures in this book since 1974 (Changabang) are taken on Olympus cameras and lenses, using Kodachrome 25 and 64 above the snowline and Kodachrome 200 below.